THE CLASS ACT BOOK

For a complete list of Global Management titles, visit our website at www.goglobalmgt.com or email us at infoGME@aol.com

THE CLASS ACT BOOK

HOW YOU CAN BECOME A CLASS ACT

Mike Pegg

First Published in 2004 by Management Books 2000 Ltd

Publishedin 2009 by Global Management Enterprises,LLC
Massachusetts, USA

ISBN 978-1-934747-41-4

Contents

Introduction

How can you develop your 'A' talent? How can you become a 'Class Act'? This is a phrase used to describe somebody who consistently does brilliant work – then adds that touch of class. Such people deliver the goods when it matters. Who do you believe demonstrates these qualities? Try tackling the exercise called A Class Act. Think of a person who you feel does great work. They can be in sports, the arts, business or any field. What do you believe they do right – especially at crucial moments? Can you follow any of these principles in your own way? This book provides practical tools that you can use to do what you do best.

Start by choosing an activity in which you can become … and want to become … a class act. How to find such fertile ground? Select one in which you experience three things: energy, ease and excellence.

- First, you get positive energy – doing it puts a spring in your step.
- Second, you feel at ease and things come relatively 'easily.'
- Third, you get independent feedback that you excel.

Bearing these answers in mind, choose your potential niche. Double-check it is one in which can be a 'Warrior-Wizard.' What does this mean? Warriors love doing the necessary grunt work. Wizards make creative breakthroughs and do great work. Choose an activity in which you combine both sets of characteristics to be a Warrior-Wizard.

"Sounds simple," you may say, "but are there any more clues to finding my talent?" One approach is to explore your positive history. You can do this by tackling the exercise later in the book called *My Successful Style*. Looking back on your life, clarify what for you have been your most satisfying 'projects.' The term 'project' can be used in its broadest sense. For example, writing an article, raising money for charity, leading a sports team, producing a play, renovating a house, launching a web site or whatever. Looking at each project in turn, can you see any patterns? How can you follow these in the future? Later we will consider how to make this happen.

So, begin by choosing a stimulating activity in which you want to become a Class Act. Then focus on five steps towards doing memorable work: **Character, Competence, Consistency** and **Creativity** – plus adding a touch of **Class**. Let's explore these steps.

● CHARACTER

Character is the foundation for success. Do you have the right drive, discipline and decision-making appetite? For example: A sales person must have the drive to hit financial targets … and the resilience to overcome rejection. An athlete must have the discipline to train every day. Do you relish making decisions in your chosen activity… especially the tough ones? On a scale of 0 to 10, how do you rate yourself as having the character required to achieve success?

● COMPETENCE

Great performers have the right strengths, strategic decision making ability and skills. What are your strengths? How can you capitalize on these talents to reach your goals? Good decision-making will be vital. When tackling a challenge, you may consider employing the Seven C Model for making decisions. Buying time to get a helicopter view of the situation, you can focus on **Calmness, Clarity, Choices, Consequences, Creative Solutions, Conclusions** and **Concrete Results**. Pursuing the right strategy will take you so far – but you will also need certain practical skills to reach your goals. How do you rate yourself as having the competence required to achieve success?

THE CLASS ACT MODEL

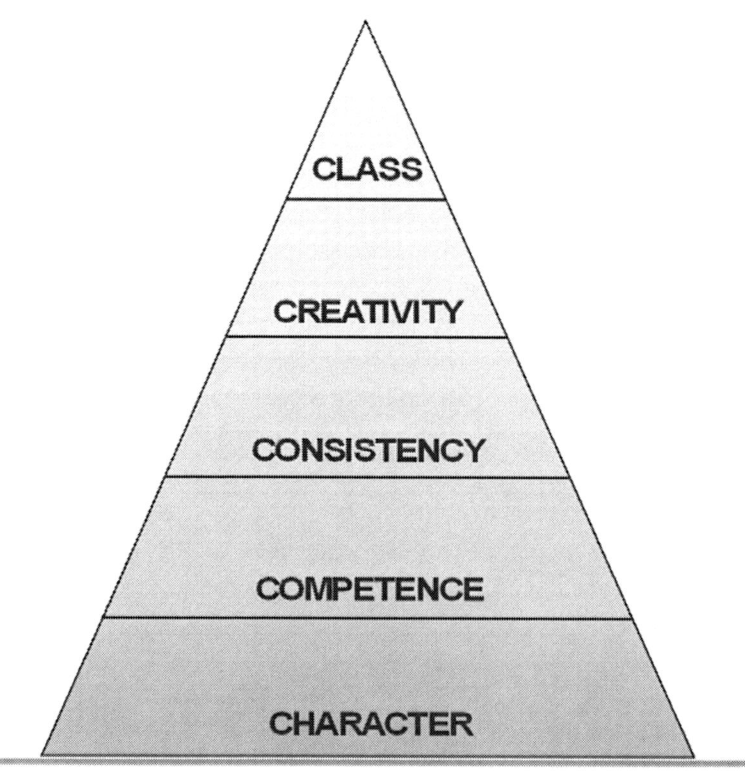

Choose an activity in which you can become a Class Act

A CLASS ACT

a) Write the name of a person who you believe is, or has been, 'A Class Act.' He or she consistently performs brilliantly and also adds that 'touch of class.' It can be somebody in sports, the arts, business or any other field.

- ____________________

b) Describe the things you believe this person does right – or did right – to be a Class Act.

- He/she ____________________
- He/she ____________________
- He/she ____________________
- He/she ____________________
- He/she ____________________

• CONSISTENCY

Great workers are positive, professional and peak performers. Overcoming personal setbacks and crises, they consistently deliver at least an 8/10. How do they maintain such high standards? Class Acts are positive by nature and focus on 'controlling the controllables.' Professional to their finger tips, they practice good habits. They do the right things in the right way every day. Proactivity is crucial. Looking ahead, great workers continually address issues that are in the Green, Amber and Red Zones. How do you rate yourself as having the ability to consistently deliver peak performances?

• CREATIVITY

Success calls for employing the right creativity at the right time to get the right results. Creativity comes in many different forms, but three themes underlie most approaches. Class Acts have the Radar and Repertoire required to deliver Results. What does this mean? First, they have great 'personal radar' in their chosen field. They quickly see patterns and the potential picture of perfection. Second, they have the professional repertoire – the strengths, strategies and skills – required to capitalize on what they see. Third, they employ their personal radar and professional repertoire to deliver positive results. How do you rate yourself as having the creativity required to succeed?

• CLASS

Class Acts demonstrate that 'touch of class' at special moments. There are three kinds of such moments.

a. *The 'creative' moment* – when you are pursuing an activity and experience an epiphany or breakthrough.
b. *The 'cherry on the cake' moment* – when you complete a task successfully and then add that 'little bit extra.'
c. *The 'critical' moment* – when you perform brilliantly in a crisis or under pressure.

Many people long for those moments, because it is when they feel fully alive. Pausing to reflect, they become very calm. Things seem to go 'slowly yet speedily.' They then take five steps towards 'climbing the mountain at the top of the mountain.' They focus on:

1. **Clarity** – they clarify the real results to achieve.
2. **Creativity** – they quickly explore all the 'conventional' and 'creative' options.
3. **Commitment** – they commit themselves to their chosen route.
4. **Concrete results** – they deliver concrete results.
5. **Class** – they demonstrate that touch of class.

Great performers enter a 'cocoon of concentration' at such moments. After settling on their chosen route, they relax, re-center and refocus. Feeling fully present, they get the right balance between focusing on the process and the prize. Putting themselves in the background, they become selfless and channel their strengths towards achieving success. They then flow, focus and finish. Sometimes the solution appears stunningly simple, but therein lies its genius. Sounds a long process, but great performers go through these stages in a split second.

Would you like to develop your talents? The following pages provide practical tools you can use to build on your strengths. You can also use many of the ideas to help others develop their gifts. Let's begin by exploring where you can become a Class Act.

CHOOSING TO BECOME

A CLASS ACT

Introduction

How can you do what you do best … and do it brilliantly? You can start by planting seeds in fertile ground. Choose an activity in which you can become — and want to become — a class act. Make sure it is one in which you experience energy, ease and excellence. First, you get positive energy — doing it puts a spring in your step. Second, you feel at ease and things come relatively 'easily.' Third, you can excel. You get a reality check — feedback from other people — that you consistently deliver As. How to identify such an activity?

Let's begin by looking back at your positive history. Can you remember a time when – even if only for a moment – you behaved like a Class Act? This could have been in your personal or professional life. You may have been making a keynote speech, launching a campaign, coaching a person, managing a personal crisis, solving a problem or whatever. Try tackling the exercise on this theme called *Being A Class Act*. Looking back at the event, what did you do right then? How can you follow these principles in the future?

> "The critical moment I recall was after being publicly attacked in a Director's meeting," said Anna. "Having been recently promoted to head the Customer Services Department, I was invited to present my strategy to the Board. Feeling nervous, I outlined my suggestions. Five minutes into the presentation, a newly arrived Director interrupted. He positioned his statement by saying, 'As the new boy, I see things with fresh eyes. So I want to drill down and challenge your argument.' The next few minutes felt more like a personal attack. Later, I was told he came from a company that had a macho culture based on 'critical questioning.'
>
> "The new Director criticized my presentation, the department and the company's customer service. Trying to stay calm, I paused to reflect. If I lost my temper, I would be playing his game. If I stayed

> silent, I would be giving in to bullying. Waiting until he had finished, I decided to stand my ground, saying: 'I understand your concerns. If you turn to the backup documentation, you will see I have outlined several ways forward ... together with the pluses and minuses. I have highlighted the recommended option, but am open to other views. What do other people think?' The Managing Director took over, saying: 'Anna has done extensive research. I think it would be good to listen to her recommendation.' The next day, the MD visited my office to apologize. Three months later the newly appointed Director left. The official explanation was he had chosen to take up another opportunity, but the real reason was his persistent bullying. Looking back to the Board presentation, I am amazed how I kept cool at the critical moment."

When did you behave like a class act? How can you follow these principles again in your personal and professional life? Let's move onto clarifying possible niche – beginning by exploring where you feel in your element.

You can clarify what gives you energy

Energy is life. When you do feel alive and excited? Try tackling several exercises on this theme. As with all the exercises in this book, you may quickly discover patterns when doing them, so just tackle those exercises that you feel are most relevant.

- The first is called *Energy*. Clarify: (a) what gives you energy; (b) what drains energy. How can you do more things that give you energy?
- Move onto the exercise called *Alive*. When do you live the 'A' life – feeling alive and alert – rather than the 'B' life – feeling bored – or the 'C' life – feeling cramped?
- A similar exercise is called *Positive Engagement*. When do you feel positively – and fully – engaged? When are you partly engaged? When are you 'pretend' engaged?
- Move onto *My Creative Fixes*. When do you get a creative fix?

Perhaps it is writing an article, building a business model, fixing a customer problem or whatever. How can you get a creative fix at least three times a day?

- Finally, tackle the exercise called *Excitement.*

"*Exciting* is not a word I use much these days," remarked one manager. "My work is interesting, but it does not light my fire." How to make this happen? Writing in *The Ageless Spirit*, Rollo May urged people to do the things they loved – otherwise the muscles wither. Confronted by individuals who doubt their own creativity, he wrote:

"What is it that you make? What is it that you do? When we think in those terms, then all of us are creative – we all do things, make things – I really think creativity is the answer to ageing, and by creativity I mean listening to one's own inner voice, to one's own ideas, to one's own aspirations. It may be social work. It may be gardening. It may be building. But it must be something fresh, something or an idea that takes fire. You are never fully satisfied ... you are always working and reworking your art, your book, your garden, whatever."

When do you feel alive? What gives you energy? When are you creative? What do you get excited about? How can you do more of these things? Let's move on to the next quality you will experience in your potential niche.

BEING A CLASS ACT

Let's explore your positive history. Can you remember a time when – even if only for a moment – you behaved like a Class Act? What were you doing right then? How can you follow these principles in the future?

The time when – even for only a moment – I behaved like a class act was:

- when I ____

____

The specific things I did right to behave like a Class Act then were:

- I ____
- I ____
- I ____

The specific things I can do to follow these principles and behave like a Class Act in the future are:

- I can ____
- I can ____
- I can ____

ENERGY

Energy is life. This exercise invites you to define the activities that: a) give you energy; b) take away energy. You are then invited to look at how you can do more of the things that give you energy.

The things that give me energy are:

- ______________________________
- ______________________________
- ______________________________

The things that drain energy are:

- ______________________________
- ______________________________
- ______________________________

The specific steps I can take to do more of the things that give me energy are:

- ______________________________
- ______________________________
- ______________________________

ALIVE: LIVING THE 'A' LIFE

This exercise invites you to clarify the activities in which you feel Alive. The 'A' Life is one where you feel alert and may gain a sense of achievement. The exercise also invites you to consider the 'B' and 'C' life – where you feel Bored or Cramped. How can you feel more alive by expanding the 'A' activities and beginning to discard the 'B' or 'C' activities? The exercise invites you consider how to make this happen.

ALIVE: The 'A' Life. The activities in which I feel alive are when I am:

- ______________________________
- ______________________________
- ______________________________
- ______________________________
- ______________________________
- ______________________________
- ______________________________
- ______________________________
- ______________________________

BORED: The 'B' Life. The activities in which I get bored are when I am:

- ____
- ____
- ____

CRAMPED: The 'C' Life. The activities in which I feel cramped are:

- ____
- ____
- ____

THE 'A' LIFE – MY ACTION PLAN

The concrete steps I can take to do more of the 'A' activities – and less or none of the 'B' and 'C' activities – in the future are:

- I can ____________________________________
- I can ____________________________________
- I can ____________________________________

POSITIVE ENGAGEMENT

Peak performers are positively engaged in what they do. When are you positively – and fully – engaged? When are you partly engaged? When are you 'pretend' engaged? This exercise invites you to clarify these situations and take whatever steps you wish to increase your positive engagement.

POSITIVELY ENGAGED. The situations in which I feel positively – and fully – engaged are when I am:

- ____
- ____
- ____
- ____
- ____
- ____
- ____
- ____
- ____

PARTLY ENGAGED. The situations in which I feel I am partly engaged are when I am:

- ____
- ____
- ____

PRETEND ENGAGED. The situations in which I feel 'pretend' engaged are when I am:

- ____
- ____
- ____

ACTION PLAN. Bearing these answers in mind, the steps I want to take are:

- to ______________________________________
- to ______________________________________
- to ______________________________________

MY CREATIVE FIXES

This exercise invites you to focus on how you can continue to live a creative life. People like to follow a passion, set positive goals and achieve positive results. They get a kick from, for example, painting a picture, training at the gym, helping a person in a one-to-one session, designing a model, writing an article, presenting a keynote speech or whatever. Many people find it is vital to get a 'creative fix' – however small – at least three times a day. This exercise invites you to focus on how you can make this happen.

The things that give me a creative fix are:

- when I ____________________
- when I ____________________
- when I ____________________

The steps I can take to do more of these things are:

- I can ____________________
- I can ____________________
- I can ____________________

EXCITEMENT

What do you get excited about? First, describe the things you find exciting, plus rate how high these score on the excitement scale. Second, describe the reasons you get excited about these things. Third, describe how you can do more of the things you find exciting.

The things I get excited about are:

1. ____

The extent to which I get excited about this is: ______/10

The reasons I get excited about this are:

- ____

The steps I can take to do this more often are:

- ____

2. ____

The extent to which I get excited about this is: ______/10

The reasons I get excited about this are:

- ____

The steps I can take to do this more often are:

- ____

You can clarify where you feel at ease

When do you feel in your element? When do you say: "This is where I was meant to be?" Actors feel at home on the stage; chefs in the kitchen; athletes in the sports arena. "I feel safe on the soccerl field," said one star player. "My troubles disappear when I am playing a game." If you wish, try tackling several exercises on this theme. *Ease* invites you to describe where you feel at home. Move on to defining where you have the natural ability to succeed in *Things Come Easily*. Finally: When do you quickly see the desired destination? When do you go 'A, B ... then leap to Z'? Clarify where you have this ability in the exercise called *Pictures of Perfection*.

> "Put me in any shop anywhere in the world and I will show you how to improve their profits," said the MD of a High Street chain. "I love the 'smell' of retail. My wife thinks I am crazy, because on Sundays I want to take her shopping. My parents owned several successful restaurants, so I grew up with traders. Put me in a formal dinner with pompous business people, however, and I feel uncomfortable. I wander down to the kitchen and talk with the chefs. We discuss how to make more money from the meal. That's where I feel at home!"

Recognizing when you are in your element is a start – but sweat is required to complete the journey. Let's explore where you translate ideas into reality.

EASE

What are the situations in which you feel 'at home'? Try to be as specific as possible with your answers.

The specific situations where I feel at ease are:

1) When I am ____________________

The reasons I feel at ease are:

- ____________________
- ____________________
- ____________________

2) When I am ____________________

The reasons I feel at ease are:

- ____________________
- ____________________
- ____________________

'THINGS COME EASILY'

What are the activities in which 'things come relatively easily' for you? Perhaps it is because you have a natural ability or have worked hard at practicing the skill. This exercise invites you to describe those activities – and the reasons why they come easily.

The specific activities in which things come relatively easily for me are:

1) When I am ______________________________

The reasons why they come relatively easily are:

- ______________________________
- ______________________________
- ______________________________

2) When I am ______________________________

The reasons why they come relatively easily are:

- ______________________________
- ______________________________
- ______________________________

PICTURES OF PERFECTION

What are the situations in which you quickly see the potential picture of perfection? You go A, B … then quickly jump to Z? This exercise invites you to describe the situations where you quickly see the desired destination.

The situations in which I quickly see the potential Picture of Perfection are:

1) When I am ________________________________

____

____

2) When I am ________________________________

____

____

3) When I am ________________________________

____

____

You can clarify where you deliver excellence

What is the activity in which you excel? When do consistently deliver As, rather than Bs or Cs? One approach is to follow your vocation. Your vocation is your calling – it is what you are here to do – and may be expressed in a recurring life-theme. The 'red thread' in your life may be, for example: helping people to develop their talents; building businesses; solving problems; making the world a better place or whatever. Your vocation remains constant. Over the years, however, you will employ different vehicles for expressing it on the road towards doing valuable work.

So how do you discover your key theme? Clues can be found in your positive history. Everybody has a pattern of success. You can find yours by tackling the exercise called *My Successful Style*. This highlights the 'What' and 'How' involved in doing stimulating work. The exercise is in three parts.

1. Looking back at your life, describe the 'projects' that for you have been both satisfying and successful. Considering each project in turn, describe what made it rewarding. (The term 'project' can be used in its broadest sense. For example: passing an exam, traveling around Europe, creating a web site, running a marathon, shipping a product and so on.)

2. Looking at these projects, can you see any patterns? If so, describe what you see as your successful style.

3. Looking to the future, describe the kind of activity, project or role where you will be able to follow your successful style.

Different people discover different patterns when doing this exercise. For example, Tom discovered his successful pattern was 'building prototypes.' He loves to create profitable new ventures in customer service. His startups include (a) introducing Italian coffee shops to the high street, and (b) launching an Internet travel service. Getting bored with maintenance, Tom recruits his successor and hands over to them within two years. He is a business pioneer whose pattern was relatively easy to find. Let's explore one that was more difficult to discover.

Jacqui attended a workshop I ran for a travel company. She led a marketing department but wanted to change direction. (The travel company invited their people to attend a career development session every two years. The aim was to encourage individuals to take charge of their careers – and it was okay to consider options both inside and outside the company. Paradoxically, the majority of participants chose to stay. Tom was one of those who crafted a niche within the business.) Tackling the *My Successful Style* exercise, Jacqui found her key theme was 'creating enriching environments.' She now runs a home design company with her husband, David Smith, a gifted carpenter. Jacqui explains her story in the *'The Birth of HomeSmiths.'* (See panel on page 35)

MY SUCCESSFUL STYLE:
Finding and following it in the future

Everybody has a successful way of working. This three-part exercise invites you to clarify your best style.

1. Looking back at your life, describe the 'projects' that for you have been both satisfying and successful. Considering each project in turn, describe what made it rewarding. (The term 'project' can be used in its broadest sense. For example: passing an exam, traveling around Europe, creating a web site, running a marathon, shipping a product and so on)
2. Looking at these projects, can you see any patterns? If so, describe what you see as your successful style.
3. Looking to the future, describe the kind of activity, project or role where you will be able to follow your successful style.

My satisfying and successful projects:

a) When I ____

The things that made it satisfying and successful were:

- ____
- ____
- ____
- ____
- ____

b) When I ______________________________

The things that made it satisfying and successful were:

- ______________________________
- ______________________________
- ______________________________
- ______________________________
- ______________________________

c) When I ______________________________

The things that made it satisfying and successful were:

- ______________________________
- ______________________________
- ______________________________
- ______________________________
- ______________________________

My Successful Style: clarifying it

Bearing in mind the patterns that have emerged, describe what you believe is your successful style. (You may, of course, have several different successful styles. For example, one when working alone, another when working with other people.)

My successful style is:

- to ______________________________
- to ______________________________
- to ______________________________
- to ______________________________

My Successful Style: following it in the future

Bearing in mind *My Successful Style*, the kind of activities or roles where I may be able to follow it in the future are:

- ______________________________
- ______________________________
- ______________________________

Jacqui Smith- The Birth of 'HomeSmiths'

As a child, I could spend hours creating room sets for my dolls, fiddling with doll's house furniture, making camps for my brother to play in or rearranging my bedroom. While I followed art and excelled at it through my childhood and teens, my school was fiercely academic. So when it came to 'A' Level choices, Art was dropped in favor of Economics, Math and German! University followed, and I gained a degree in Economics and Math. Having little clue of what I wanted to do, I found myself in sales and marketing, which is where I stayed for some years.

Feeling unfulfilled with my work, job changes ensued, but I was never really addressing the root problem. Sales and marketing were not playing to my strengths. This left a whole host of skills and, more importantly, passions untapped. Outside work I was continuing with more creative pursuits, such as designing room schemes for myself and for friends and family. But I never thought of doing this for a living, telling myself: 'I'm not trained in Interior Design – how could I make money from this and why would anyone take me seriously?' Despite constant encouragement from friends, I remained unhappy in the corporate world.

Several years ago, I went on a two-day workshop aimed at helping people to make a living doing what they loved. Focusing on my passions, talents, dreams and goals threw up a common theme that simply read as 'creating enriching environments.' I then met my now husband David, a cabinet maker. He had always wanted to run his own business, yet possessed none of the required sales, marketing or organizational skills. Within months of meeting, we were engaged. We also knew then that we would one day set up on our own. David continued to design and make furniture in the short to medium term. In the longer term, however, he wanted to get more involved in bigger interior design projects. I wanted to help people enrich their living environments with color and texture-plus take on the challenge of running a business. A brainstorm and a bottle of wine later 'HomeSmiths' was born. The name offers so much flexibility in terms of what we offer our clients – from furniture making and interior design, through to anything that enhances one's living environment.

The response from our immediate network was tremendous. Not only did people believe in the proposition, but truly believed in David's and my ability, through our combined talents, to deliver. Starting the business when our first child was 4 months old, people thought we were mad – but staying in our old roles was so much more frightening! It has been hard work and we are still a young business, but we are building our reputation. We work together incredibly well. Some projects involve both of us designing the furniture as well as the overall room scheme; other clients simply want to commission a piece of furniture.

We pride ourselves on our quality of product and service. Although bespoke furniture is not exactly a regular purchase, we have already had three clients return to us for further work. One lesson I learned on the workshop was to network but, most of all, to give something back to people in your network. So true and such a simple and cost effective way to grow a business! I am evangelical about doing work you love and, as a mother, will certainly encourage my children to follow their natural paths in life and work.

You can read more about Jacqui and David's work at **www.homesmiths.co.uk**

"Discovering my successful style is fine – but how can I tell where I excel?" you may ask. Try tackling the exercise called *Delivery: The 3 Ds*. Looking at your chosen activity, rate yourself on Drive, Detail and Delivery. Drive – how high is your drive? Detail – how high is your attention to detail? Delivery – how high is your ability to consistently deliver the goods? Make sure you score at least 8/10 on each of the 3 Ds. But what if you cannot find your successful style – or are just starting out on your career?

You can clarify your possible niche – the project, people and place

Here is another guide to choosing the activity in which you can perform at your best. Try tackling the exercise called *My Possible Niche*. Focus on the kind of project, people and place that you find stimulating. Why? In the old days, individuals were attracted by the reputation of a particular business and said things like: "I want to join that company." Sometimes it worked; other times they discovered the company did not practice what it preached. So how to choose the right place? Looking back in later life, individuals frequently recall doing an inspiring project with an inspiring person … or people who gave them encouragement. So it is good to go in that order: project, people and place. Let's consider these three dimensions.

• PROJECT

Describe the kind of project which you find stimulating – and where you also do good work. You may feel alive when selling; creating a web site; solving conflicts; building prototypes; recovering customer service problems; facilitating workshops; coaching; writing articles; making presentations; retailing; encouraging people; painting pictures; leading teams or whatever. Describe the kind of project where you work best.

DELIVERY: The 3 Ds

People who do brilliant work score highly on the 3 Ds. This exercise invites you to rate yourself in these areas of Drive, Detail and Delivery. Make sure you score a total of at least 24/30.

The activity in which I want to become a Class Act is:

- ______________________________

Drive

The extent to which I have a strong drive and desire to do this activity is:

______/10

Detail

The extent to which I have attention to detail when doing this activity is:

______/10

Drive

The extent to which I deliver the goods when doing this activity is:

______/10

• PEOPLE

Describe the kind of people who you find stimulating – both customers and colleagues. Do they have a certain personality style? Are they positive, negative or a mixture? Are they decision makers, middle managers or front-liners? Are they: (a) architects – who just want the big picture and headlines; (b) builders – who want to know the implementation plans; (c) craftsmen – who focus on the fine details? Are they intuitive, logical or a mixture? Do they have certain values or professional standards? Do they give an immediate response or are they more introverted, taking time before responding? Do you prefer working with those in a specific field, such as retail, engineering or high tech? Describe the people with whom you work best.

• PLACE

Describe the 'place' – the culture and environment – that gives you energy. This may be a 'physical' place, a 'psychological' place, or a mixture of both. You may feel stimulated working in a particular culture, such as a high tech company, a service industry, a shop, a hotel or wherever. Where do you feel at home and at ease? Describe the kind of place where you work best.

Finally, combine the answers from your project, people and place. Begin to clarify your potential niche. This is the 'What.' *Do not worry yet about 'How' to get paid.* We will explore the commercial aspects later in the book.

MY POSSIBLE NICHE: Choosing the project, people and place

How to choose the right niche? This exercise invites you to focus on four things.

1. **Project**. Describe the characteristics of the kind of project you find stimulating. (The stimulation factor should be at least an 8/10).
2. **People**. Describe the characteristics of the kind of people – both customers and colleagues – you find stimulating.
3. **Place**. Describe the characteristics of the 'place' – culture and environment – you find stimulating.
4. Bearing these things in mind, describe what may be your potential **niche**.

PROJECT – The kinds of projects that I find stimulating are ones where:

- ____________________
- ____________________
- ____________________
- ____________________
- ____________________

PEOPLE – The kind of people that I find stimulating are:

- ____________________
- ____________________

- ______________________________
- ______________________________
- ______________________________

PLACE – The kinds of places – culture and environment – I find stimulating are:

- ______________________________
- ______________________________
- ______________________________
- ______________________________
- ______________________________

POSSIBLE NICHE – Bearing these answers in mind, the possible niche where I may do my best work is:

- ______________________________

____

____

You can choose where you want to become a Class Act

Time to finalize your chosen activity. Start by tackling the exercise called *My Potential Routes Towards Becoming A Class Act*. Draw the different options you have for doing fine work. For example: Option A is: __________ Option B is: __________ Option C is: __________ Clarify the pluses and minuses of each route – then rate their attractiveness. Looking at the alternatives: Which provides the greatest chance of success? Rate the probability of becoming a Class Act in each activity – then settle on your chosen route.

Sometimes this exercise helps to clarify your professional priorities. Tackling it in 2002, for example, I identified three routes. Option A was to write books that enabled people to build on their strengths. Option B was to do one-to-one mentoring with certain kinds of people. Option C was to run super-team workshops for highly focused project teams. Several other routes were possible, but the probability rating of doing fine work was only 7/10. Bearing the top three options in mind, I gradually shifted my diary to create more time for writing. Today this occupies around 140 days a year, mostly on Fridays, Saturdays and Sundays. The one-to-one mentoring has increased – but with the people with whom I work best. The super-team work is now around 10 workshops a year – rather than 20 – for dedicated teams who want to achieve a specific picture of perfection.

What are your options? Clarify the potential routes, then concentrate on the most attractive option. Complete the exercise called *My Chosen Activity – The Activity In Which I Want To Become A Class Act*. Describe the reasons you believe you can excel, plus the benefits – both for yourself and other people. Be super specific about your niche. The more specific you are, the greater the chances of success. Then move onto a reality check.

MY POTENTIAL ROUTES TO BECOMING A CLASS ACT

This exercise is in several parts. (1) Make a map of the possible activities in which you might become a Class Act. For example: Options A: to ____, Option B: to ____ etc. (2) Describe the pluses and minuses of each option. (3) Rate how attractive each of these options is to you. Do this on a scale 0 to 10. (4) Rate the probability of your becoming a Class Act in this activity.

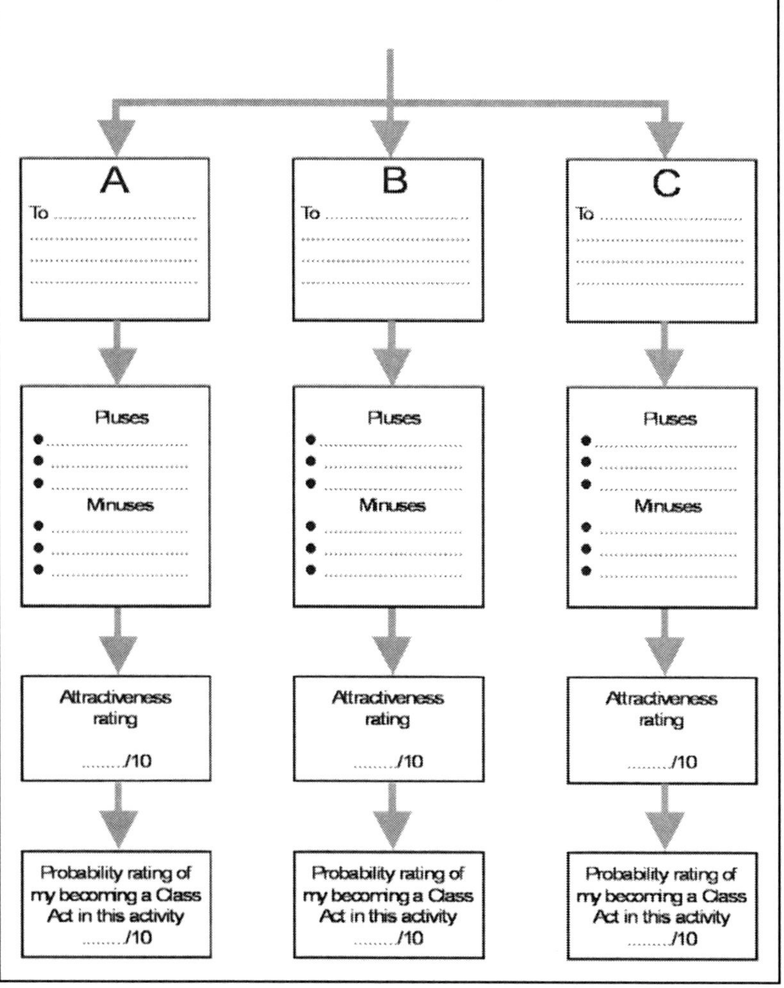

MY CHOSEN ACTIVITY:

The activity in which I want to become a Class Act

The activity in which I feel I can become – and want to become – a Class Act is:

- ____

____

The reasons I believe I can become a Class Act in this activity are:

- ____
- ____
- ____

The benefits of becoming a Class Act in this activity will be:

For myself	For other people
• __________________	• __________________
• __________________	• __________________
• __________________	• __________________

You can double-check you have chosen the right niche

How to check if you are on the right road? Make sure the activity is one where: (1) you score highly on Energy, Ease and Excellence, (2) you score highly on the Caring Dimension and (3) you can be a Warrior-Wizard. Let's explore these dimensions.

1. You score highly on Energy, Ease and Excellence

Looking at your chosen activity, check to what extent you will: (a) get positive **Energy**; (b) feel at **Ease**; and (c) consistently deliver **Excellence**. Rate each of these on a scale 0 to 10. Make sure the total score is at least 24/30. 'Energy' is crucial. You should experience positive energy just thinking about the activity, saying: "I can't wait to do it again."

2. You score highly on the Caring Dimension

Looking at your chosen activity, do you really care about the outcome? Anything below 8/10 is a danger signal. Why? Peak performers care about their work. They also look for meaning in the end result – which calls for more than making extra profits for shareholders. If the corporate tasks they are asked to do lack excitement, they reframe these to find some meaning – even if it is simply paying the mortgage. Adopting this attitude carries them through the day, but wears thin over the years, which can lead to disillusionment.

"The caring part strikes a chord," said Ben, a freelance IT contractor. "Two years ago, I worked three days a week for a High Street retail chain. Initially they made outside suppliers feel welcome and called them 'partners.' The chain then held a big corporate conference to launch two initiatives called 'Excellence & Effectiveness.' Sounded fine – but the implementation was confusing. Employees were told to strive for excellence but, on the other hand, instructed to cut

> unnecessary costs. For example, the overnight hotel subsidy for 'partners' was to be halved from $70 to $35. My contact told me to: 'Stop staying in hotels and find good bed and breakfast accommodation.' Company directors continued to have expensive 'Away Days,' however, and fly first class. Cutting corners became a way of life, eventually leading to the IT systems crashing. Updating the security software became essential, but the managers became paralyzed, refusing to make a decision. Eventually I stopped caring about my job and the company. Now I work for a business that aims to practice what it preaches."

Try tackling the exercise on this theme called *The Caring Dimension*. First, clarify to what extent you care about the outcome of your chosen activity. Second, clarify the reasons you care. Third, clarify how to put yourself into more situations in which you care. Then move onto one final check.

3. You can be a Warrior-Wizard

Warriors work hard and have the resilience to overcome setbacks. Wizards have the wisdom and imagination to make creative breakthroughs. Class Acts embrace both sets of qualities and are Warrior-Wizards. They love the *grunt work* – which provides the springboard for the *great work*. Looking at your chosen activity, how would you rate yourself as a Warrior-Wizard? Score yourself on a scale 0 to 10. Describe the reasons you gave this score. Describe the steps you can take to improve as a Warrior-Wizard.

ENERGY, EASE AND EXCELLENCE

How to judge whether you have chosen an activity in which you can be a Class Act? One way is to rate yourself in the areas of Energy, Ease and Excellence. This exercise invites you to take that step. Aim for at least 24/30.

The activity in which I want to become a Class Act is:

- ______________________________

ENERGY – The extent to which I experience positive energy when doing this activity is:

_____/10

EASE – The extent to which I feel at ease and things come to me relatively 'easily' when doing this activity is:

_____/10

EXCELLENCE – The extent to which I consistently deliver As when doing this activity is:

_____/10

THE CARING DIMENSION

Class Acts really care about their chosen activity – otherwise they can become sloppy. This exercise invites you to clarify three things. First, the extent you care about the outcome of the activity in which you wish to become a class act. (Anything below 8/10 on the caring scale is a massive warning sign.) Second, the reasons you care about it. Third, the steps you can take to put yourself in more situations where you really care.

The extent to which I care about the activity in which I want to become a Class Act is:

_____/10

The reasons I care about this activity are:

- ______________________________
- ______________________________
- ______________________________

The steps I can take to put myself in more situations that I really care about are:

- ______________________________
- ______________________________
- ______________________________

BEING A WARRIOR-WIZARD

Warriors work hard and have the resilience to overcome setbacks. Wizards have the imagination to make creative breakthroughs. Class Acts embrace all these qualities and, in their chosen activity, are Warrior-Wizards. This exercise invites you to clarify to what extent you embrace these qualities.

The activity in which I want to become a Class Act is:

- ____________________

WARRIOR-WIZARD – The extent to which I am a Warrior-Wizard when doing this activity is:

_____/10

The reasons I give this score are:

- ____________________
- ____________________
- ____________________

The steps I can take to improve as a Warrior-Wizard in this activity are:

- ____________________
- ____________________

You can rate yourself as a Class Act

How will you know when you become a Class Act? What will be happening? What is your picture of perfection? Where are you now? Where do you want to be? How can you make the journey? Great performers have the right character, competence, consistency and creativity – then add a touch of class. Score yourself in each of these areas in the exercise called *Rating Myself As A Class Act*. Do this on a scale 0 to 10.

'Maybe I am not following the instructions properly,' said one person, 'because I am giving myself very high scores. I scored 9/10 on Character, Competence and Consistency, plus 7/10 for Creativity and 6/10 for Class. Can that be right? Am I doing something wrong?'

You may also score highly. Why? When applying their specific talent, gifted people quickly reach 7/10. But then comes the real test – because the climb from 7 to 10 is exponential. Going from 7 to 8 is like moving from being County Champion to becoming National Champion; 9 is becoming European Champion; 10 is becoming World Champion. That is a massive climb.

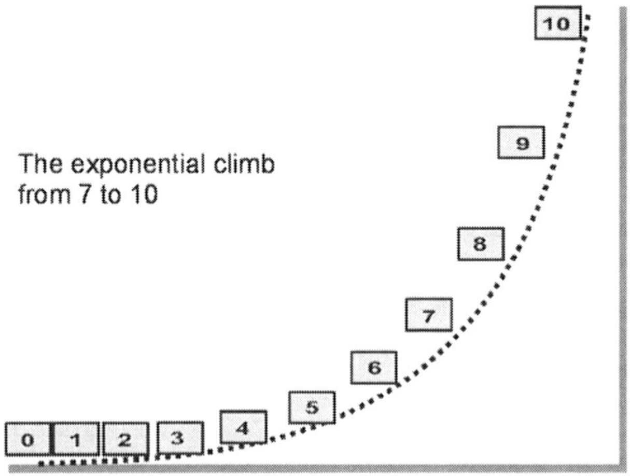

How can you improve your ratings? The following pages provide tools you can use to become a Class Act. After *Rating Myself as a Class Act*, let's take a deeper look at the first step – **Character**.

RATING MYSELF AS A CLASS ACT

How do you rate yourself in the activity where you want to be a Class Act? On a scale 0 to 10, rate yourself in the areas listed below.

The activity in which I want to become a Class Act is:

- ______________________________

The ratings I would give myself in this activity are:

CHARACTER

Having the drive, discipline and decision making appetite required to succeed. _____/10

COMPETENCE

Having the strengths, strategic decision making ability and skills required to succeed. _____/10

CONSISTENCY

Having the consistency of positive approach, professionalism and peak performance required to succeed. _____/10

CREATIVITY

Having the right kind of creativity required to succeed.

_____/10

CLASS

Having the ability to be demonstrate that touch of class at special moments. _____/10

CHARACTER

Introduction

Have you got the character – the drive, discipline and decision making appetite required to succeed? A sales person must have the desire to hit financial targets. An athlete must have the discipline to train in bad weather. A leader must relish making decisions-especially the tough ones. Which decisions do you enjoy taking? Which do you find more difficult? Desire is the starting point – but it is not enough. Everybody is bound to experience setbacks. Resilience is crucial. How do you bounce back from disappointments?

This section explores how you can continue developing the personality required to become a class act.

Looking at your chosen activity, how strong is your drive? Let's revisit the score you gave yourself regarding character. How did you rate yourself on a scale of 0 to 10? Which qualities do you have already? Which can you develop? Going a little deeper, try the exercise called Ch*aracter: Drive, Discipline and Decision Making Appetite*. Rate yourself on each of these themes. Make sure you score at least 8/10 on drive. What if you score less? Revisit your passion and translate it into a clear purpose – because passion and purpose generate great energy.

You can ensure you have the right drive

What gets you out of bed in the morning – your mission, your mortgage or a combination of both? People who follow their vocation find that their drive gets stronger as they get older. One person said: *"Maybe it is because I am 70 and acutely aware of mortality. During my 50s, I experienced my first real illnesses and realized that everything is 'temporary.' Now I enjoy each day. Persistence is one of my main assets. I want to keep on working and will be happy to die with my boots on."* Athletes show a similar drive in the latter stages of their career. Every competition is a bonus and they enjoy each moment. People experience something else as they get older – the desire to pass on knowledge to future generations.

Maggie Khun was such a person who showed remarkable drive. She acted as an enterprising model for thousands of people around the world. During the early 1970s, she and five friends reached the compulsory retirement age of sixty-five. Disgusted at the way America devalued its older people, they created the Grey Panthers. *"There's a new kind of energy that comes from late in life, a new freedom,"* said Maggie. She mobilized older people to claim their rights and show what they could offer society. Her initiative attracted global attention and created a world-wide membership of the Grey Panthers. Writing in The Ageless Spirit, Maggie declares:

"I am having – and I say this quite candidly and gratefully – a glorious old age. Sure, I have arthritis; sure I have very severe arthritis in my hands. It is very hard for me to open things and turn off a light switch; there are lots of things I cannot do. I have arthritis in my knees, too, and at times it's very painful and I have difficulty walking. But there's nothing wrong with my head, thank goodness, and nothing wrong with my spirit.

"Old folks need to be mentors for the young," said Maggie, *"and the young need old folks just as much as we need them.:* She created housing co-operatives where old and young people shared accommodation. Older people offered their life-experience and wisdom, younger people offered their energy and practical skills. Maggie believed in passing on knowledge from generation to generation.

CHARACTER

The activity in which I want to become a Class Act is:

- ____

The characteristics I believe somebody must demonstrate to be a Class Act in this activity are:

- to ______________________________________
- to ______________________________________
- to ______________________________________

The characteristics I already have are:

- to ______________________________________
- to ______________________________________
- to ______________________________________

The characteristics I need to add or improve are:

- to ______________________________________
- to ______________________________________
- to ______________________________________

CHARACTER: Drive, Discipline and Decision Making Appetite

How can you judge whether you have the character required to become a Class Act? One approach is to start by clarifying the activity in which you want to excel. Then rate to what extent you have the personal drive, discipline and desire to make tough decisions in your chosen field. A good guideline is to ensure that you have a total score of at least 80% – a minimum of 24/30.

The activity in which I want to become a Class Act is:

- ______________________________

DRIVE – The extent to which I believe I have the personal drive required to succeed in my chosen activity is:

______/10

DISCIPLINE – The extent to which I believe I have the personal discipline required to succeed in my chosen activity is:

______/10

DECISION MAKING APPETITE – The extent to which I relish making the tough decisions required to succeed in my chosen activity is:

______/10

Returning for a moment to Maggie Kuhn, she also said, *"I believe that there has to be a purpose and a goal to life. The secret of thriving and surviving is to have a goal. Having a goal is absolutely essential, because it gives you the energy and the drive to do what you must do, and to get up when you feel like staying in bed... I have plenty of goals! On my eightieth birthday, in fact, I vowed to myself that I would do something outrageous at least once a week, and for the past few years I've been able to live up to that promise."*

Do you ever feel possessed by your drive? *"I was born with the ability to play the saxophone,"* said one jazz musician, *"so I feel an obligation to use my talent."* Try tackling the exercise on this theme called *Drive: A Sense of Duty*. First, describe your drive. Second, describe the sense of duty you have to this drive. Third, describe how you want to translate this into action. *"But, isn't there a price to pay if you have a strong drive?"* somebody may ask. Yes, there are pluses and minuses – but there is also a price to pay for not following your passion. The key is to 'become friends' with your 'possession.' Channel your drive in a way that benefits both yourself and other people.

Desire is crucial – but determination is required to overcome disappointments. Are you resilient? How long does it take you to bounce back from setbacks? Looking back on you life, can you remember a time when you recovered successfully? What did you do right then? How can you follow similar principles in the future? Try tackling the exercise called *Drive: The Delights And Disappointments*. Clarify how you can build on the positives and overcome any difficulties. *"Ninety-nine percent of the time I experience pleasure,"* said one person, *"but I also encounter problems. I love my work, however, and accept the whole package."* People often learn from setbacks and the 'breakdown' leads to a breakthrough. Pain leads to wisdom and produces greater achievements. Let's move onto the next step.

DRIVE: A sense of duty

DRIVE – The drive I have is:

- to ____________________

____

DUTY – The sense of duty I feel towards following this drive is:

- to ____________________
- to ____________________
- to ____________________

DELIVERY – The way I want to follow this drive is:

- to ____________________
- to ____________________
- to ____________________

DRIVE: The delights and disappointments

DRIVE – The drive I have is:

- to ______________________________

____

DELIGHT – The delights – the pleasures – I get from following this drive are:

- ______________________________
- ______________________________
- ______________________________
- ______________________________

The specific things I can do to build on and enjoy these delights are:

- ______________________________
- ______________________________
- ______________________________

DISAPPOINTMENT – The disappointments I may experience when following this drive are:

- ____________________________________
- ____________________________________
- ____________________________________

The specific things I can do to manage these disappointments are:

- ____________________________________
- ____________________________________
- ____________________________________

DELIGHT AND DISAPPOINTMENT – My Action Plan

The specific things I can do to build on the delights and manage the disappointments are:

- I can ________________________________
- I can ________________________________
- I can ________________________________

You can ensure that you have the right discipline

Success calls for developing good habits. The dancer warms up before practicing; the scientist studies the latest research; the athlete eats the right food. "But I am not disciplined," somebody may say. But is this true? People may be self-managing when doing what they love, but not in other areas of their lives. 'Billy Elliott' was disciplined when dancing, but not when getting up for school. Actors may be authoritative on stage but disturbed in their personal lives. Looking at your chosen activity, which disciplines come to you naturally? Which can you develop? Which can you 'buy-in' from outside? You don't have to do everything. If you are running your own business, for example, you may generate more money by doing what you do best, rather than spending time doing your book keeping. Tackle the exercise on this theme called *Discipline*. Describe how you can do the right things in the right way every day.

Rollo May believed people could improve their discipline by capitalizing on their 'Prime Times.' Writing in *The Ageless Spirit*, he explained:

"I stay in my studio each day for four hours, but the last hour and a half isn't worth very much. It was hard for me to accept, but what can I do? All I can do is make the most of the creative time I've got. So for two and a half hours I'm moving marvelously; the rest of the time I'm simply fiddling around. But I find joy in fiddling too. I have to accept the fact that I'm not a God. I have to accept my destiny. I have to accept the fact that I can only do creative work for a few hours a day, but that does not diminish one iota the joy I get from those two hours."

When do you feel most energetic? How can you protect these hours and 'catch the wave'? Try tackling the exercise called *My Prime Times*. Capitalizing on these times can improve your productivity.

DISCIPLINE

The activity in which I want to become a Class Act is:

- ________________________________

The disciplines that come to me naturally when doing this activity are:

- to ______________________________
- to ______________________________
- to ______________________________

The disciplines that I need to improve or 'buy in' are:

- to ______________________________
- to ______________________________
- to ______________________________

The steps I can take to be disciplined and do the right things in the right way everyday are:

- to ______________________________
- to ______________________________
- to ______________________________

MY PRIME TIMES

When are your prime times — the times of the day you have most energy? This exercise invites you to clarify, protect and capitalize on your prime times.

The times of the day when I have the most energy are:

- 1 ______________________________
- 2 ______________________________
- 3 ______________________________

The steps I can take to protect and capitalize on these prime times are:

- 1 ______________________________
- 2 ______________________________
- 3 ______________________________

You can ensure you have the right decision-making appetite

People love making decisions in their area of expertise – especially the tough ones. They say: "Give it to me. I will make the decision." Raymond Blanc insists on controlling the quality of food in his restaurant. Jane Tomlinson enjoys shaping her strategy for raising charity money. Steven Spielberg wants to be in charge when directing his films. Decision making is a drug. The more you do it, the more you want to do it. People are happy to be accountable, providing they also have the autonomy and authority required to deliver the goods.

"My role is to recommend whether or not criminals previously considered 'mentally ill' can be released into the community." said Stephen, a psychiatrist. *"It sounds odd, but I enjoy taking these decisions. The responsibility can be daunting, because making mistakes can cost lives. Tabloid newspapers and politicians are also continually piling on pressure. Morally, however, should we be allowed to let a recovered person rot in jail? Somebody must decide. I am confident in my ability to carry out my duty properly – both from the medical and moral point of view. People say they don't envy my role, but it is a job I feel is necessary in our society."*

Which decisions do you enjoy taking – and which are more difficult? Tackle the exercise called *My Decision Making Appetite.* First, describe the decisions you like taking – even the tough ones. Second, describe the decisions you don't like taking or find difficult. Third, describe what you can do (a) to make more of the decisions you enjoy taking and (b) to bolster your ability to take the tougher decisions. We will explore the whole issue of making choices further in the next chapter when considering Strategic Decision Making Ability.

MY DECISION MAKING APPETITE

Decision making is one of the keys to becoming a Class Act. Bearing in mind the activity in which you want to do great work, this exercise invites you to describe three things: (1) the kind of decisions you do enjoy making in this activity-including the tough ones; (2) the kind of decisions you don't enjoy – or find more difficult and (3) the specific things you can do (a) to take more of the decisions you like taking and (b) to bolster your ability to take the other decisions.

The activity in which I want to become a Class Act is:

- ______________________________

The decisions I DO enjoy taking in this activity – even the tough ones – are:

- ______________________________
- ______________________________
- ______________________________
- ______________________________
- ______________________________
- ______________________________
- ______________________________

The decisions I DON'T enjoy making – or find more difficult – in this activity are:

- ____________________
- ____________________
- ____________________
- ____________________

DECISION MAKING – The specific things I can do -

to take more of the decisions I do enjoy taking are:

- to ____________________
- to ____________________
- to ____________________

to bolster my ability to take the decisions I find more difficult are:

- to ____________________
- to ____________________
- to ____________________

Sara Hall is another person who loves taking charge of her destiny. Writing in *Drawn To The Rhythm: A Passionate Life Reclaimed*, she describes her personal odyssey. Trapped in a loveless marriage, she followed the path taken by many people who reclaim their lives. Sara took charge of her feelings, took charge of her future and, eventually, took charge of her finances. Sculling was the passion that rekindled her joy, but first she had to regain her autonomy. So what happened? Sara was 42. She had three children, a fine house and a husband whose money meant she could devote herself to the family – but the marriage was broken. Sara's epiphany came unexpectedly. Driving past the harbor one day, she spotted a lone rower on the water. Entranced, she later wrote:

"One rower, I'll never know who, one boat so gorgeous, so lyrical, so piercing that I pulled over onto the shoulder and stopped the car, my heart pounding ... In the quiet thrust of the boat, the sweet swing of the sculler, I saw everything I wanted to be, everything I always had been beneath the sensible dresses and the sorrow. Found in that moment the mission of these hands, this body, this heart."

Sara suddenly discovered her drive – to learn to scull – which became a metaphor for being reborn. Discipline was required. She woke before dawn, trained on the water, and was back to feed her family breakfast when they rose at 6:30. Sculling fed Sara's decision making appetite. Out on the water, she had autonomy and did not need to ask for permission. *Drawn To The Rhythm* catalogues Sara's setbacks and triumphs. She reclaimed her life, won championship medals and was acclaimed on national TV. She eventually moved on from her marriage, but sporting 'success' brought another battle. She fell in love with the medals – the badge collecting – rather than the joy of sculling. Sara looked in the mirror and did not like her reflection. She was allowing the medals to define her self-esteem. Feeling she had exchanged one slavery for another, she decided to take charge of her destiny.

Swimming out into the sea one morning, Sara kissed each medal goodbye — then let them slip one-by-one into the deep. She writes: *'Then I was free. My medals were in a safe place. A year later almost to the day I won the World Masters Games in the single shell.'* Why? Did it have anything to do with letting go? Sara explains how, when racing under pressure, she had been urged to relax. *'Hold each oar as though you are holding sparrows,'* rowing coaches say. *'Hold them too loose and they fly away. Hold them too tight and you kill them. Hold the sparrows in your hands.'* Sara relearned to flow, focus and finish. She relearned to love the process as much as the prize. Paradoxically, this resulted in even more success. Sara demonstrated the character required to be a Class Act.

Conclude this chapter by completing the exercise on *Character: My Action Plan*. Describe three things you can do to continue developing the character required to succeed in your chosen activity.

After the exercise, we can move onto the next step towards becoming a Class Act – **Competence**.

CHARACTER: MY ACTION PLAN

The steps I can take to continue developing the character required to succeed in my chosen activity are:

- to ____

____

____

- to ____

____

____

- to ____

____

____

COMPETENCE

Introduction

Great performers have the strengths, strategic decision-making ability and skills required to achieve success. What are your top strengths? How can you use these to reach your goals? Good decision making will be crucial – so how do you make decisions?

You may wish to employ the Seven C Model when tackling challenges – focusing on **Calmness, Clarity, Choices, Consequences, Creative Solutions, Conclusions** and **Concrete Results**. Strategy will take you so far – but you will also need certain practical skills. This section considers the strengths, strategic ability and skills required to achieve your picture of perfection.

Let's revisit the rating you gave yourself regarding competence. How did you score yourself on a scale of 0 to 10? What is the reason you gave this score? Looking at your chosen activity, which qualities do you believe somebody must demonstrate to succeed? Which qualities do you have already? Which can you develop? Which can you 'buy-in'? Let's explore how to boost your competence.

You can develop your strengths

Peak performers go beyond employing just one of their talents. They often combine several strengths to create something special. Bob Geldof put together his musical network and persuasive powers to mobilize Live Aid. Anita Roddick combined her ecological awareness with business savvy to create The Body Shop. Muhammad Ali maximized his physical and psychological skills to out-psyche opponents in the boxing ring, where he aimed to 'float like a butterfly and sting like a bee.' Such people follow a process that is common in the world of inventions. Breakthroughs often come from fusing together two or more previously unconnected things. The Sony

Walkman, for example, emerged from the founder's desire to listen to music while also walking. Pioneers combine their strengths to achieve their goals – and sometimes they use them to help others to succeed.

'Sounds okay, but can this approach work for a person early in their career?' somebody may ask. Yes, let's explore how this works in practice.

Mikael Larson was 17 when he attended a workshop I ran for unemployed young people in Northern Sweden in 1982. (For reasons that will become apparent, he now calls himself Mike.) Despite being so-called 'dropouts,' the youngsters responded well and I invited them to do each draw 'My Ideal Life.' Returning to the school hall after the coffee break, I found Mike scaling a vertical wall. *'I enjoy climbing,'* he said. *'Look at my poster. It shows what I plan to do in my life.'*

Mike may have found school boring, but was certainly ambitious. He had drawn himself climbing a mountain and, at the bottom, was a mother and child. *"My ideal life would be to earn money climbing,"* he explained, *"but this may be difficult to do full time. During the summer I work as a mountain guide, but I have also invented safety devices for climbers. One day I will have my own company ... and also raise a family."* Fire burned behind Mike's eyes as we resumed the workshop. Two months later, I was sent a newspaper photograph. Showing Mike climbing a church spire, the article reported he had started a company called 'High Service.' Carrying his mountaineering gear from village to village, he specialized in cleaning church spires. He photocopied the articles, then sent these to the next village, asking if they needed their spire cleaned. Mike seemed to be on the march, but I lost track of him for several years.

COMPETENCE

The activity in which I want to become a Class Act is:

- ____________________

The competence I believe somebody must demonstrate to be a Class Act in this activity are:

- to ____________________
- to ____________________
- to ____________________

The abilities I already have are:

- to ____________________
- to ____________________
- to ____________________

The abilities I need to add or improve are:

- to ____________________
- to ____________________
- to ____________________

STRENGTHS, STRATEGIC DECISION MAKING AND SKILLS

How can you judge whether you have the talent required to become a Class Act? One approach is rate to what extent you have: (a) the natural strengths; (b) the strategic decision making ability; and (c) the practical skills. This will provide a basis for considering whether you have the competence to become a Class Act in your chosen field.

The activity in which I want to become a Class Act is:

- ______________________________

STRENGTHS – The extent to which I believe I have the natural skills required to succeed in my chosen activity is:

______/10

STRATEGIC DECISION MAKING – The extent to which I believe I have the strategic decision making ability required to succeed in my chosen activity is:

______/10

SKILLS – The extent to which I believe I have the practical skills required to succeed in my chosen activity is:

______/10

Ten years later, I returned to run another workshop in Sweden. Two young people introduced themselves at the start of the program. "Mike Larson sends his regards,: they said. :We work for the company he founded called 'Act Safe.' We have 20 employees and specialize in making safety clothing for mountaineers, firefighters and steeplejacks. Business is great, and we supply retailers all over Europe." During the past 40 years, I have been fortunate to work with many people who have demonstrated drive. Mike showed this at an early age but, like many entrepreneurs, had not fitted into the school system. He had combined three major talents. First, his climbing knowledge. Second, his inventiveness and ability to improve climbing equipment. Third, his commercial 'nous.' Mike combined his assets to become a real peak performer.

> Writing this book in 2004, I tried to find Mike. Searching the net, I discovered he had sold his company but founded another that creates climbing maps for mountaineers. Doing international work, he now signs his emails 'Mike,' which is easier for non-Swedes to say, rather than Mikael. He responded to my email when dashing to the airport to climb in Italy. He wrote: "I was poor, then rich, and now am poor again. But I am happy." Mike and his partner have seven children. They are buying a bus to travel around Europe, climb mountains, map the routes and educate their children about different cultures. Mike has created his niche. His company, Coronn, can be found at: **www.coronn.com**

What are your top talents? How can you fuse these together to create something special? Try tackling the exercise on this theme called *My Strengths*. Clarify how you can combine your talents to help yourself or other people to succeed. Let's move on to the next step.

MY STRENGTHS

Peak performers often combine several strengths to achieve success. Sometimes they do this to achieve their own goals. Sometimes they do it to help others to succeed. First, describe your top two or three strengths. Second, describe how you can combine these strengths to either (a) help yourself to succeed, or (b) help other people – such as potential sponsors – to succeed.

My three top strengths are:

- I can ______________________________
- I can ______________________________
- I can ______________________________

The ways I can combine these strengths to help myself or others to succeed are:

- I can ______________________________
- I can ______________________________
- I can ______________________________

You can develop your strategic decision-making ability

How many decisions have you made today? People make decisions every minute. They choose their attitude, their behavior and, to some extent, the consequences. How do you make decisions in your personal and professional life? One approach is to follow 'The Seven Cs For Strategic Decision Making': **Calmness, Clarity, Choices, Consequences, Creative Solutions, Conclusions** and **Concrete Results**. You can take these steps to get a helicopter view of the possible options and then choose the best route towards your goals. Let's explore how this works in practice.

Carole had reached a crossroads. Three years of traveling as a 'road warrior' had taken its toll. Living in the North, she worked as the Regional Manager for High Street stores in the Midlands. Before taking the role, Tony, her partner, and she agreed that promotion from Store Manager to Regional Manager was a giant career step – plus a 50% pay rise. Failure to take the job would mark her down as 'unambitious.' Carole had taken the role – which meant driving 40,000 miles a year, staying four nights a week in hotels and working 14-hour days. Successfully hitting her targets in the first three years produced a huge bonus, which she and Tony spent on holidays – something they needed to reconnect in their relationship. Returning to the road this autumn, Carole encountered several warning signs.

"I'm constantly tired," reported Carole. *"Starting out at 5 a.m. on Monday morning, I do not return home till Friday midnight. The face-to-face contact with store managers is great, but I don't enjoy the headquarters meetings. The company has marked me out as a positive role model for women, but I am not sure if I want to pay the price. Three events last week brought matters to a head. Tony and I had a row on Sunday night, the company offered me a bigger Regional Manager's job in the South East and then, returning home at 10:00 p.m. on Friday, my car tire burst. Standing on the M6 hard shoulder, while making an emergency call to the AA, certainly focuses the mind, especially on a cold November night. It's time to consider my future."*

Let's look at how the Seven Cs can be used to tackle this challenge.

Step 1: CALMNESS

Carole began by taking time out to reflect. She needed to helicopter above events and gather information. *"Getting time to see the big picture sounds obvious, but that is not always easy,"* said Carole. *"People push you to make a quick decision."* She set aside two hours one Sunday morning to talk with Tony. They considered the way forward-which involved moving on to the next step.

Step 2: CLARITY

Clarity is crucial. Good decision makers define the challenge and phrase it in positive terms. They ask themselves: "What are the Real Results I want to achieve?" They clarify the 'What' before moving onto the 'How.' If somebody has several goals – which is often the case – they list these in order of priority. (Sometimes this might include short-, medium- and long-term goals.) Looking six months into the future, Carole clarified her picture of perfection. By then she wanted:

(a) to have regained her energy
(b) to be doing a hands-on retail job that was both stimulating and satisfying
(c) To be living with Tony in the North
(d) To be coaching people and making a positive difference in her work
(e) To be reasonably well paid.

Quality of life issues were hitting Carole and Tony. Both earned high salaries, but life had become greyer. Weekends once provided a sanctuary, but were now spoilt by outside pressures. Carole began gearing up on Sunday afternoon for her Monday morning journey down the M6. She moved onto the next step.

STRATEGIC DECISION MAKING: The Seven C Model

People can use the Seven C model when making strategic decisions. They can focus on:

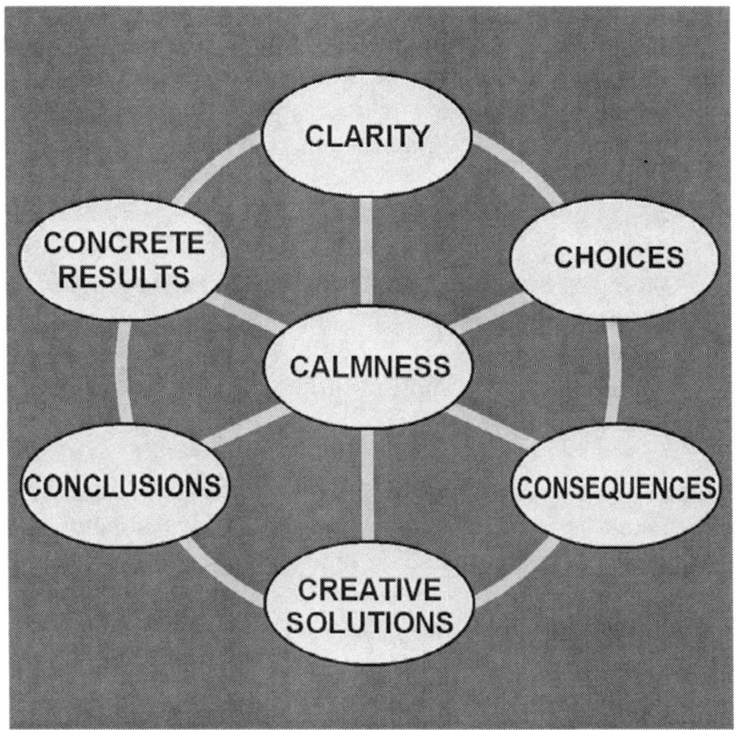

Step 3: CHOICES

Good decision makers brainstorm all the possible options. Some ideas may be non-starters, but it is good to get them out on the table, just to show they have been considered. Carole outlined the possibilities, which included:

a. continuing her present Regional Manager role in the Midlands
b. taking the role of Regional Manager in the South East – then for Tony and herself to relocate in the South
c. changing company and becoming a Regional Manager in the North
d. reverting back to her first love-being a 'hands-on' General Manager in a store
e. setting up her own company and hiring herself out as a Project Director – for example, using her expertise to help companies set up new stores
f. doing something completely different – though not sure what this would be.

"Staying in the North is important to Tony and me," said Carole. *"Both sets of parents are getting older, so we want to be around if anything goes wrong."* She moved onto the next stage of the model.

Step 4: CONSEQUENCES

Good decision makers clarify the pluses and minuses of each route – and the attractiveness of each option. One key point to bear in mind: sometimes there are not 'good' or 'bad' decisions – there are just consequences. Great leaders often base their decisions on the consequences of each option, not the options themselves. Carole outlined the consequences of each route.

a) Continuing her present Regional Manager role in the Midlands

Pluses: Good salary; 'status'; climbing the 'career ladder'; rewarding work with some general managers.

Minuses: Exhausting; being a road warrior destroys home life; trying to get things done 'through' 20 store managers brings mixed results – there is not enough time to devote to real coaching; headquarters meetings are frustrating.

Attractiveness Rating: 6/10

b) Taking the role of Regional Manager in the South East – then for Tony and herself to relocate in the South.

Pluses: Higher salary; more decision making authority; the next step to be deputy MD?

Minuses: Relocating – which we don't want to do; more headquarters meetings.

Attractiveness Rating: 4/10

c) Changing company and becoming a Regional Manager in the North. (I have been approached by head-hunters to join several retail companies.)

Pluses: More money; more time at home; new challenge.

Minuses: Leaving my present company; span of control – maybe being the Regional Manager for up to 30 store managers; still spending time on the road.

Attractiveness Rating: 7/10

d) Reverting back to my first love-being a 'hands-on' General Manager in a store.

Pluses: Love 'retail as theatre'; coaching my own team; less travel.

Minuses: Seen as a downward step; less money; possible boredom – but would find exciting campaigns to implement.

Attractiveness Rating: 7/10

e) Setting up my own company and hiring myself out as a Project Director. For example: Using my expertise to help companies to set up new stores.

Pluses: Being my own boss; staying in the North; exciting projects.

Minuses: Uncertain income.

Attractiveness Rating: 7/10

f) Doing something completely different ... though not sure what this would be.

Pluses: Could be exciting.

Minuses: What would I do?

Attractiveness Rating: 1/10

Carole felt equally attracted to options c, d and e – but none really stood out. She and Tony moved onto the next step.

Step 5: CREATIVE SOLUTIONS

Decision makers now employ their imagination. They ask questions like: 'What is the best part of each option? Is it possible to combine these into a new option? Are there any other possibilities?' After 15 minutes spent kicking ideas around, Carole started putting together the best parts of each option. She would like:

- to be based in the North
- to run a big, flagship store
- to devote time to coaching people in the store
- to pass on her expertise – preferably through making training

videos and setting up a sales academy
- to also coach people who were starting new stores – which would be more satisfying than being a daily operations 'cop'
- to, if possible, retain her present level of income.

Carole considered how to craft such a role. She also clarified the business benefits, because this was the only way the company would consider such an option.

Step 6: CONCLUSIONS

Good decision-makers often take time out at this point to reflect on the possibilities – and the implications. They reflect, re-center and refocus on their picture of perfection, then choose their way forward. (Sometimes, of course, they may wish to pursue parallel options.) This then leads on to committing themselves to a clear action plan.

Carole settled on her chosen route – running a flagship store in the North, plus coaching. Where might this be possible? The Liverpool and Leeds stores already had good managers. But the Manchester store's future was more uncertain. Built on a Retail Park in the 80s, it needed a massive revamp. She would relish the challenge. What if this option did not work out? Carole would take her proposal to a rival company. Tony and she agreed that, if both approaches failed, she would set up her own business. She was street-wise. Carole planned to approach her MD, involve him in the process and look for a 'win-win.' Professional to the core, there was no way she wanted to back him into a corner. She recommitted herself to her chosen route – then moved onto the final step.

Step 7: CONCRETE RESULTS

Good decision-makers create specific action plans, implement these successfully and get concrete results. Carole asked to see the MD. Thanking him for the South East Regional Manager offer she explained that, for personal reasons, it was important to spend more time in the North. She wanted to stay with the company, however, and explained her options – together with the pluses and minuses. Carole asked if he could see any other possibilities.

The MD's view was that, providing she continued with the Midlands Regional Manager for the next four months – holding the fort over Christmas – he would love her to revitalize the store in Manchester. Money was not an issue (he knew she had been headhunted). Carole could retain her present salary, providing she could provide onsite coaching sessions for managers opening new stores. Certainly this would involve nights away from home, but more likely to be three, rather than sixteen, a month.

Would it mean the end of her upward career? Perhaps – but badge collecting and board meetings were not nirvana. Carole would have many opportunities to make her mark, especially if she could launch a successful sales academy. The MD underlined that he wanted her to stay in the company and aimed to get a 'win-win.' Carole felt more at ease. She knew the company would honor its promise and looked forward to revamping the Manchester store. Ringing the AA from the M6 had brought matters to a head. Running a flagship store – that also acted as a training centre – was where she could become a Class Act.

The Seven Cs sounds a long process. People learn to go through the stages quickly, however, and it becomes second nature. If you wish, you can use the model to tackle a real-life challenge in the exercise called *Strategic Decision Making*. Let's move onto the next stage.

STRATEGIC DECISION MAKING:
How you can use the Seven C model

The following pages provide a framework for practicing the Seven C model. Start by listing the challenges you face in your life and work – then focus on one challenge you would like to tackle. Go through the steps and settle on how you can deliver concrete results.

The key challenges that I face in my life/work at the moment are:

- how to ______________________________
- how to ______________________________
- how to ______________________________

Bearing these in mind, the challenge I would like to explore is:

- how to ______________________________

Step 1: CALMNESS

If appropriate, ask yourself, how can I stay calm? How can I help others to stay calm? How can I 'helicopter' and get an overview of the situation? (You may already feel calm enough … if so, move onto the next step.)

The specific things I can do to stay calm are:

- to ______________________________
- to ______________________________
- to ______________________________

Step 2: CLARITY

Looking at the challenge, ask yourself, what are the Real Results I want to achieve? If you wish to achieve several results, list these in order of priority.

The *Real Results* I want to achieve are:

1. to ____

2. to ____

3. to ____

Step 3: CHOICES

Ask yourself, looking at the real results I want to achieve, what are the possible options I have for moving forward?

The possible options are:

Option A – to ____

Option B – to ____

Option C – to ____

Step 4: CONSEQUENCES

Ask yourself, looking at each option in turn, what are the pluses and minuses of each option? On a scale of 0 to 10, how attractive is each option?

The Consequences Of Each Option Are:

Option A – to ________________________________

PLUSES	MINUSES
• ____________________	• ____________________
• ____________________	• ____________________
• ____________________	• ____________________

Attractiveness Rating: _____/10

Option B – to ________________________________

PLUSES	MINUSES
• ____________________	• ____________________
• ____________________	• ____________________
• ____________________	• ____________________

Attractiveness Rating: _____/10

Option C – to ____________________________________

PLUSES	MINUSES
• ____________________	• ____________________
• ____________________	• ____________________
• ____________________	• ____________________

Attractiveness Rating: _____/10

Step 5: CREATIVE SOLUTIONS

Ask yourself, what is the best part of each option? Could we put these together into a new option? Are there any other possible options?

The possible creative solutions are:

- to ____________________________________
- to ____________________________________
- to ____________________________________

Step 6: CONCLUSIONS

Bearing in mind the answers to all these questions, ask yourself: What is the conclusion? Which route do I want to follow? (Or: What parallel options do I want to follow?) How can I commit myself to following this route?

The route I want to commit myself to following is:

- to ______________________________

____

Step 7: CONCRETE RESULTS

Ask yourself, what are the actual steps I must take to deliver the concrete results?

The steps I can take to deliver the required concrete results are:

- to ______________________________
- to ______________________________
- to ______________________________

You can develop your skills

Strengths and strategy will take you so far – but you must also have certain skills to achieve success. If you are running your own business, for example, you must manage your time, offer quality products, get customers, make clear contracts, do fine work, send invoices, get paid, pay bills, manage the finances, complete the tax returns, develop new products and so on. Paul Hawken helped millions of budding entrepreneurs to develop these skills with his 1980s American public television series called *Growing A Business*. He followed many principles associated with 'Right Livelihood,' the concept of doing work that helps – rather than harms – people and the planet. Here are some of his tips.

• Provide quality products that help customers to succeed

Even in a recession, says Paul, customers will pay for quality products delivered in a quality way. He adds: *"Remember that in business you are never trying to 'beat' the competition. You are trying to give your customer something other than what they are receiving from the competition. It is a waste of time and energy trying to beat the competition because the customer doesn't care about that rivalry."* Give superb service, and help the customer to be successful.

• Recreate something that has been lost

People are attracted to nostalgia, so recreate something which they believe has been lost forever. The friendly small town bank; the reliable mail-order firm; the honest garage; the quality ice-cream shop; the traditional cheese store; the aromatic coffee shop; the company that fixes mistakes without complaint. Adding the 'personal touch' will eventually translate into the profitability column.

• Use your imagination

"Businesses suffer from a lack of imagination, not capital," says

Paul. Too much money is worse than too little. Having money tends to replace creativity. Companies without money are hungry; they must dream, imagine and improvise. Companies awash with money try to buy solutions. They lavish vast amounts on consultants, lawyers, clever accountants, publicity agents and marketing studies. Cash and creativity are both necessary, but make sure you balance them properly.

• Be responsible

'Be honest and ethical,' is a key principle. But how to translate this laudable approach into practice? 'Pay suppliers as soon as they have done the work,' is the first rule. Why? Traders have completed the job and have a family to feed, so pay their invoices immediately. You then have a clean bill of health – not being in debt – and help traders who may wait ages for bigger companies to pay their debts.

• Do your own book keeping for the first year

Why? Even if you hate accounting, keeping the books will give you a 'feel' for the money – how it comes in and how it goes out. Once this knowledge is in your gut, you will make better financial judgments. If you subsequently outsource the book-keeping and tax returns, keep an eye on the incomings and outgoings. Make sure it tallies with your gut feel for the financial management.

• Develop your problem-solving skills

"Businesses will always have problems," says Paul, who once searched for magic solutions. He believed that, providing he read more books by business gurus, one day he would find business nirvana. Enlightenment would make all his problems disappear. The truth hit him one sunny autumn afternoon:

"I had my nirvana, all right, but it was the opposite of what I had been seeking. On that pretty afternoon, the actual truth finally struck me: I would always have problems. In fact, problems signify that the

business is in a rapid learning phase. The revelation was liberating. I couldn't understand why other people hadn't told me this earlier."

Problems create either energy or paralysis, says Paul. Good professionals make problems interesting and mobilize people's energies to find solutions. Poor professionals present problems as threats, criticisms or things to be ignored. They issue memos, blame others or say it is the customer's fault. Get used to problems – they are an eternal part of everyday business life.

● Develop 'tradeskills'

Business people require talent, tenacity and tradeskills. Talent is the ability to do great work. Tenacity is the ability to sweat and overcome setbacks. Tradeskills help to get sufficient funding for the services you provide. People who demonstrate trade skills have the following characteristics.

- ✍ They are crystal clear on what they offer to customers.
- ✍ They recognize how what they offer can help potential customers to be successful.
- ✍ They keep in touch with customers, understand the challenges such people face and help them to achieve success.
- ✍ They invest masses of upfront time in getting to know and helping the potential customers – even though they have not yet got the business. (They also know when to cut their losses.)
- ✍ They recognize that potential customers need to cross an emotional line before they decide to buy. They respect this line, rather than push or alienate the person.
- ✍ They get the right balance between offering customers 'commodities' and 'customized solutions.'
- ✍ They know how to charge for what they offer and ask for funding – money.
- ✍ They deliver great service to customers.
- ✍ They keep networking, reach out to more potential customers and develop future business opportunities.

"Most of us know whether we possess tradeskill," says Paul, *"If you haven't got it, the best thing to do is to recognize this and plan your life and career accordingly."* You can still build a business, but you will need to complement your assets with other people who have trade skills.

Try tackling the exercise on this theme called *The Entrepreneurial Test*. Clarify to what extent you have the appropriate talent, tenacity and trade skills. Paul concludes by tackling an old myth.

"The common wisdom holds that entrepreneurs love to take risks," says Paul, *"that's mostly hype."* Entrepreneurs are like mountain climbers. They set specific goals, clarify their strategy and anticipate ways to tackle problems. Onlookers think the mountaineer is gambling, but the climber would risk more by not following his dream. *"Once the entrepreneur has seen how to create a product or service to meet demand,"* says Paul, *"much of what the outsider perceives as risk in the situation is erased."* On the other hand, he adds, risk-avoiders do not always make good entrepreneurs.

Looking at the activity in which you want to excel, which skills must you master? These may be practical, problem-solving or other professional skills. Which skills can you develop? Which can you 'buy in' from outside? Conclude this section by completing the exercise on *Competence: My Action Plan*. Reflect back on your strengths, strategic decision making ability and skills. Bearing these qualities in mind, describe how you can develop your competence. After these two exercises, we will move onto the next step towards becoming a class act – **Consistency**.

THE ENTREPRENEURIAL TEST

Business people require talent, tenacity and trade skills. Talent is the ability to do great work. Tenacity is the ability to sweat and overcome setbacks. Tradeskills is the ability to get sufficient funding for the services you provide. This exercise invites you to rate your ability in these three areas.

TALENT – The extent to which I have the talent required to succeed is: ______/10

The things I can do to improve this rating are:

- to ____

TENACITY – The extent to which I have the tenacity required to succeed is: ______/10

The things I can do to improve this rating are:

- to ____

TRADESKILLS – The extent to which I have the tradeskills required to succeed is: ______/10

The things I can do to improve this rating are:

- to ____

COMPETENCE: MY ACTION PLAN

The steps I can take to continue developing the competence required to succeed in my chosen activity are:

1. to ______________________________

____

____

2. to ______________________________

____

____

3. to ______________________________

____

____

CONSISTENCY

Introduction

Great workers are positive, professional and peak performers. Overcoming personal setbacks and crises, they consistently deliver at least an 8/10. How do they maintain such high standards? Positive by nature, they focus on 'controlling the controllables.' Professional to their finger tips; they keep doing the right things and develop good habits. Staying proactive, they look ahead and tackle issues that are in the Green, Amber and Red Zones. Great workers manage their physical, psychological and productive energy. They are then ready to deliver the goods when it matters. This chapter explores how you can consistently produce peak performances.

Let's revisit the score you gave yourself regarding Consistency. How did you rate yourself on a scale of 0 to 10? What are the qualities you believe somebody must demonstrate to be consistent in your chosen activity? Which qualities do you have? Which can you improve? Try tackling the exercise called *Consistency – The 3 P Test*. How do you rate yourself as being positive? How do you rate your professionalism? How often do you deliver peak performances? Let's explore how to boost these scores.

You can continue to be positive

Alexander Calder, the painter, said: *"I had the good fortune to be born happy."* Jane Tomlinson may or may not have been born happy – but she embodies fighting spirit. Diagnosed with breast cancer at the age of 26, the mother of 3 children threw herself into raising money for charity. She underwent a mastectomy – but found the cancer had spread to her lungs and bones. Doctors said she had a few months to live, but 12 years later she was still running marathons, using them as vehicle for sponsoring Cancer Research. Since first being diagnosed, she has cycled on a tandem with her brother from John O'Groats to

Land's End; completed two London Marathons; been awarded the MBE; raised over £100,000 for Cancer Research. There are three lessons we can learn from such people.

1. They have a positive attitude

Positive people define themselves in terms of their strengths, rather than their sicknesses. They say: *"I am this person with these talents and these goals ... I am not an illness. It is my body and my life. I will take charge of my future and concentrate on my real priorities."* They believe true wealth lies in appreciating their assets – their health, relationships and talents. Some people fail to realize their good fortune until it has gone. They then say: *"Oh, I wish things could be as they were before."* Try tackling the exercise on this theme called *My Assets*. Resilient people also clarify what they can do, rather than what they can't do. If you wish, try tackling the exercise called *My Positive Attitude: Controlling The Controllables*. Describe (a) the things you can control in your life and work – such as your attitude, professionalism and so on, (b) the things you can't control, such as other people's opinions, and (c) how you can build on what you can control and manage what you can't. Let's move onto the next quality demonstrated by such people.

2. They put themselves into 'Positive Circles' rather than 'Negative Circles'

Following the Zen belief that 'everything is food,' they spend time with the people – and in the places – that are encouraging. What does this mean in practice? Several years ago, I mentored Jody, a senior manager. At the first meeting, she talked about the barriers she faced that caused stress in her life. Six months later, at the third meeting, she arrived dressed in bright colors, whereas previously she had worn grey and black. Jody was enjoying life and appeared calm. My reaction was: 'What happened?'

She explained, *"During our first session, you mentioned something I had read in books, but felt was too simple: 'People spend time in positive circles or negative circles.' The first circle involves being in positive relationships where you get positive responses and positive results. The second circle involves being in negative relationships where you get negative responses and negative results. I had put myself in negative circles. At work, for example, I concentrated on trying to influence unmotivated people, kidding myself that, if I discovered the magic key, I could achieve a turnaround. But I became enmeshed in a spider's web that sapped energy.*

"So I put myself into positive circles. In my professional life, I switched to running projects with enthusiastic people who worked hard to succeed. In my personal life, I spent time with people who gave me energy. Previously I had spent 90% of my time in negative circles, 10% in positive circles. Now it is the other way round. If energy-drainers at work ask for help, I outline the ground rules by saying: 'Yes, I am happy to talk if we can work on finding solutions.' They also have to step into the positive circle. Now I feel calmer and yet more alive."

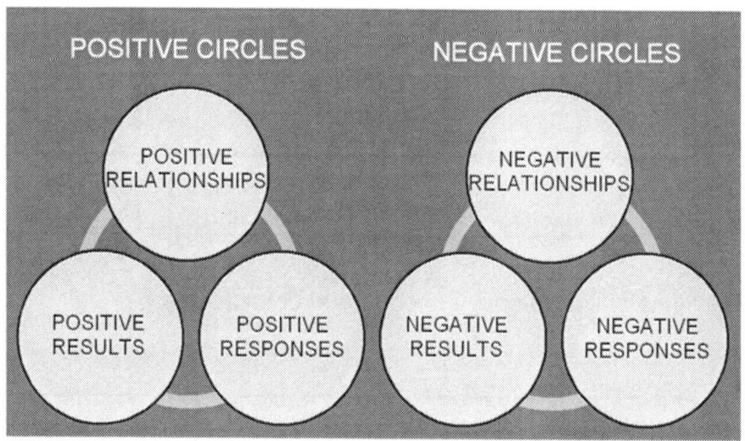

How can you put yourself in circles where you give and get positive energy? If you wish, tackle the exercise called *Positive Circles*. Then, we can move on to the next quality shown by resilient people.

CONSISTENCY

The activity in which I want to become a Class Act is:

- ______________________________

The kinds of consistency someone must demonstrate to be a Class Act in this activity are:

- to ______________________________
- to ______________________________
- to ______________________________

The kinds of consistence I already have are:

- to ______________________________
- to ______________________________
- to ______________________________

The kinds of consistency I need to add or improve are:

- to ______________________________
- to ______________________________
- to ______________________________

CONSISTENCY: THE 3 Ps

Great performers consistently demonstrate three qualities in their chosen activity. (They do not always demonstrate these qualities elsewhere.) First, they are Positive. They have a positive attitude to their work. They demonstrate this in their interactions with other people – both customers and colleagues. Second, they are Professional. They consistently behave in a professional way. This also includes being proactive – looking ahead, taking initiatives and shaping the future. Third, they consistently deliver Peak Performances. They always score at least 8/10. This exercise invites you to rate yourself in each of these areas.

The activity in which I want to become a Class Act is:

- ______________________________

POSITIVE ATTITUDE – The extent to which I consistently demonstrate a positive attitude when doing my chosen activity is:

_____/10

PROFESSIONALISM – The extent to which I consistently behave professionally when doing my chosen activity is:

_____/10

PEAK PERFORMANCES – The extent to which I consistently deliver at least 8/10 when doing my chosen activity is:

_____/10

MY ASSETS

Describe what you see as your personal and professional assets. For example: Your health, relationships, talents, drive, possessions, money and so on. People often find they have many more assets than they imagined.

The assets I have are:

- ____________________
- ____________________
- ____________________
- ____________________
- ____________________
- ____________________
- ____________________
- ____________________

MY POSITIVE ATTITUDE:

Controlling the controllables

Peak performers focus on 'controlling the controllables' in their life and work. This exercise invites you to focus on three things. First, describe the thing you can control in your life and work. Second, describe the things you can't control. Third, describe how you can do to build on what you can control and manage what you can't control.

CAN CONTROL – The things I can control in my life and work are:

- I Can Control ______________________________
- I Can Control ______________________________
- I Can Control ______________________________
- I Can Control ______________________________
- I Can Control ______________________________
- I Can Control ______________________________
- I Can Control ______________________________

CAN'T CONTROL – The things I cannot control in my life and work are:

- I Can't Control ______________________________
- I Can't Control ______________________________
- I Can't Control ______________________________

CONTROLLING THE CONTROLLABLES – The specific things I can do to build on what I can control and manage what I can't control are:

- I Can ______________________________
- I Can ______________________________
- I Can ______________________________
- I Can ______________________________
- I Can ______________________________

POSITIVE CIRCLES

POSITIVE CIRCLES – The things I can do to put myself in positive circles are:

- to ____________________
- to ____________________
- to ____________________

NEGATIVE CIRCLES – The things I can do to avoid putting myself in negative circles are:

- to ____________________
- to ____________________
- to ____________________

POSITIVE CIRCLES: ACTION PLAN – The specific things I want to do to put myself in positive circles – and avoid negative circles – are:

- to ____________________
- to ____________________
- to ____________________

3. They get positive results

How many successes have you already had today: 3, 5, 10? Success breeds self-confidence and provides energy to tackle difficult challenges. The injured athlete, for example, draws a map showing the road to full fitness. Starting from their destination, they pick a date in the future when they aim to compete for medals. Working backwards, they chart the milestones along the way. Breaking this down into long-, medium- and short-term plans, they set themselves daily goals. Putting this map on the wall, they then tick off daily achievements, which generate a sense of success.

'Sounds okay, but what if I am self-critical,' somebody may say. How can a person develop positive rather than negative scripting?

During the early 1970s, I ran a therapeutic community for teenagers who had locked themselves into negative circles. Suffering abuse in childhood, they inflicted harm on themselves or other people. How to break the cycle? The community had tough rules – the teenagers needed to take responsibility for their actions – but we also encouraged them to develop their strengths. They filled in something called *My Right Book*. Every day they wrote (a) *Three Things I Have Done Right Today*, and (b) *Two Things I Can Do Even Better Tomorrow*. Based on realistic feedback from themselves and other people, they built on their successful patterns and tackled areas for improvement. They then became more self-managing.

Try the exercise called *My Right Book* for yourself.

MY RIGHT BOOK

Three things I did right today:

- I ____

____

- I ____

____

- I ____

____

Two things I can do even better tomorrow:

- I can ____

____

- I can ____

____

You can continue to be professional

"Dave is the most professional player I have ever worked with, which is why I signed him to be captain," said one top soccer coach. *"Taking over this under-achieving team, I needed a role model and talisman. He fits the bill perfectly."* What makes Dave so super-professional?

- ✍ He arrives at the ground at 8:45, after dropping the children off at school. After getting changed, he approaches the coaching staff for an overview of the day's training.
- ✍ He is always first onto the pitch, leads the stretching and makes sure everybody is ready for the 10:00 start. (One rising star once arrived at 10:05 and, with the coach's blessing, Dave sent him back to the dressing room.)
- ✍ He is a commanding player, a great talker and organizer, and continually encourages people in the team.
- ✍ He keeps himself fit. Weighing in at the end of one season, he tipped the scales at 180 pounds. Weighing in before the following preseason training, he was 179 pounds.
- ✍ He spends two afternoons a week visiting local hospitals or doing other community work.
- ✍ He is always polite to referees and never contests decisions, preferring instead to get on with the game. He also attended a referee's course to understand their point of view.
- ✍ He has attended business leadership courses – plus gaining all the relevant coaching badges – to prepare himself for coaching a team.
- ✍ He has also supplemented the team's standard media training by hiring his own media coach.

Let's return to the activity in which you can be a Class Act. Try tackling the exercise called *Professionalism*. Describe the specific things you can do to be super-professional. For example: be on time for meetings; make clear contracts; return customer calls promptly; fulfill your promises. Proactivity is also crucial. Great performers aim to make things happen, rather than let things happen to them. They like to feel in control and ahead of the game. How to put this philosophy into practice? Try tackling the exercise called *Staying Proactive: The Green, Amber and Red Zones*.

- **The Green Zone**: Describe the things that are going well at the moment. How can you build on these successes?
- **The Amber Zone**: Describe the things that are going okay, but there may be danger signs. How can you tackle these issues?
- **The Red Zone**: Describe the things that are not going well or where there is pressure. How can you turn around these issues?

Professionals believe it is vital to 'do the day job.' Getting the basics right provides the platform for taking the next step.

PROFESSIONALISM

How can you be super professional in your work? This exercise invites you to describe the specific things you can do to consistently deliver superb results.

The specific things I can do to be super professional in my work are:

- to ______________________________

____

- to ______________________________

____

- to ______________________________

____

- to ______________________________

____

- to ______________________________

____

STAYING PROACTIVE:
The Green, Amber and Red Zones

THE GREEN ZONE: The things that are going well at the moment

The things that are in the Green Zone at the moment are:

- ____________________
- ____________________
- ____________________

The steps I can take to build on these things are:

- ____________________
- ____________________
- ____________________

THE AMBER ZONE: The things that are going okay, but there may be warning signs

The issues that are in the Amber Zone at the moment are:

- ______________________________
- ______________________________
- ______________________________

The steps I can take to tackle these issues are:

- ______________________________
- ______________________________
- ______________________________

THE RED ZONE: The things that are not going well or where I am under pressure

The issues that are in the Red Zone at the moment are:

- ____
- ____
- ____

The steps I can take to tackle these issues are:

- ____
- ____
- ____

You can continue to be a Peak Performer

How can you consistently do great work? *"That is the challenge I am facing at the moment,"* said Rosie, the MD of a software company, *"and I am not sure if it is in my present role."* Rosie has an unconventional background. Growing up in a northern town, she found school boring, but she loved working alongside her father. Rebelling against social expectations, Rosie became one of the country's first female engineering apprentices. Sailing through her apprenticeship, she eventually moved on to set up her own software firm. Selling the business after five years, she backpacked around the world. After she returned home, head hunters persuaded her to take the MD role. Rosie always performs brilliantly when working with customers.

"Bizarre as it sounds, I love tackling customer complaints," she says. *"Problems are a challenge and, being an engineer, I like making things work. Recovering a bad service situation can transform somebody into a customer for life."* Rosie adopts the Three As approach when turning around customers.

- ✍ **APOLOGIZE** – Say sorry. Simple but necessary if you are to move forward with the customer.

- ✍ **ACCEPT** – Accept the customer's point of view, because their perception is right for them. Gather specific information about what happened to create the problem.

- ✍ **ACT** – Act to solve the problem and, as far as possible, work to get a 'Win-Win.' Then implement actions to make sure similar problems don't happen in the future.

"Winning back customers is exhilarating, but we should have satisfied them in the first place," says Rosie. *"Right now I spend too much time in internal meetings, which is not stimulating. Customer situations are where I feel in my element. Perhaps I should return to running my own small business."*

Peak performers are alive and alert in critical situations. Managing their energy properly, they are 'fully present' and deliver the goods when it matters. How good are you at your managing your physical, psychological and productive energy? This calls for following three rules.

Step 1: You can manage your physical energy

Sleep for at least six hours a night and eat a good breakfast, is the time honored advice. Jim Loehr and Tony Schwartz, the authors of *The Power of Full Engagement*, offer many such suggestions for managing physical energy. They also advise eating food that releases energy slowly, preferably taking nutritional snacks every 90 minutes. As we considered earlier, another key is to make good use of your 'Prime Times' – the hours when you have most energy. Climbing any mountain is arduous, so take time out to relax, re-centre and refocus. Results require proper rest and recovery. Getting an overview enables people to make better quality decisions. On a scale of 0 to 10, how well do you manage your physical energy? How can you improve this score?

Step 2: You can manage your psychological energy

How to maximize your psychological energy? Peak performers focus on their passion, purpose and picture of perfection – this puts a spring in their step. As we mentioned earlier, they spend time in 'positive circles,' working with customers and colleagues who are energy givers. They are proactive, stay ahead of the game and find creative solutions to challenges. On a scale of 0 to 10, how well do you manage your psychological energy? How can you improve this score?

Step 3: You can manage your productive energy

'Do what you do best' is the motto. Employ your 'A' talent, rather than your 'B' or 'C' talent. Follow your successful pattern. Focus on the key strategies that will give you the greatest chance of success –

and practice superb priority management. Get the right balance between doing the Great Work and Grunt Work. Looking at your work, clarify the tasks you want to (a) drive, (b) delegate or (c) ditch. When I doubt, ask: 'Is this activity giving me energy?' If not, spend time with the people, and on the activities, that provide stimulation. On a scale of 0 to 10, how well do you manage your productive energy? How can you improve this score?

PEAK PERFORMANCE:
Managing my energy

This exercise invites you to explore how you can manage your physical, psychological and productive energy.

PHYSICAL ENERGY – The extent to which I make good use of my physical energy is: _____/10

The steps I can take to improve my physical energy are::

- I can ______________________________
- I can ______________________________

PSYCHOLOGICAL ENERGY – The extent to which I make good use of my psychological energy is: _____/10

The steps I can take to improve my psychological energy are::

- I can ______________________________
- I can ______________________________

PRODUCTIVE ENERGY – The extent to which I make good use of my productive energy is: _____/10

The steps I can take to improve my productive energy are::

- I can ______________________________
- I can ______________________________

DRIVE, DELEGATE AND DITCH

There are only so many tasks you can concentrate on fully – so priority management is crucial. Looking at your work, this exercise invites you to clarify the activities you want to drive, delegate – to a safe pair of hands – and ditch.

DRIVE – The things I am going to drive are:

- ____
- ____
- ____

DELEGATE – The things I am going to delegate are:

- ____
- ____
- ____

DITCH – The things I am going to ditch are:

- ____
- ____
- ____

You can do a performance health check

'My ratings tell me that I am a peak performer,' said one manager, *'but I don't yet feel like a class act. Is that possible?'* Yes. A ruthless business leader may produce huge company profits, for example, but fail to demonstrate the human qualities shown by a class act. Bearing this in mind, do you personally feel on the right road? Let's explore one way you can check.

People often take five steps towards doing great work. They focus on:

1. **Passion** – they follow their passion.
2. **Purpose** – they translate their passion into a clear purpose.
3. **Professionalism** – they are super professional.
4. **Problem Solving** – they find positive solutions to challenges.
5. **Peak Performance** – they consistently deliver great performances.

Try tackling the exercise on this theme called *The Peak Performance Health Check*. Rate yourself on each of the five steps. Make sure you score at least 8/10 on passion and purpose. Why? People can deliver on professionalism, positive solutions and peak performance, but will run out of energy if they do not score highly on the first two steps. What if this happens for you? One approach is to return to the first rungs of the ladder. Find ways to follow your passion and create a clear purpose.

Rosie did the *Peak Performance Health Check* – and decided to transform her career. She returned to her first love – building – and one year later explained her decision. *'The Health Check confirmed what I already knew. I functioned well at the top part of the ladder – professionalism, problem solving and peak performance. But felt like I one of those cartoon characters running madly a few feet above the ground. Peddling fast – and appearing to be successful – I was not feeling satisfied. So I revisited my passion. Turning on the television one night, I sat transfixed watching people renovating houses. My feeling was: "I can make a better job of renovation." So I bought and refurbished a small flat in Manchester, selling it at a profit. Now I have my own business again, acting as a broker running renovation projects for house buyers. Now I feel fulfilled seeing a finished product and also satisfying customers.'*

Are you on the right road? If not, revisit the activity in which you want to be a class act. Dare to be even more specific in choosing your niche. Make sure it is one that is stimulating. Conclude this section by completing the exercise *Consistency: My Action Plan*. Describe three things you can do to continually achieve high standards – then go onto next stage, **Creativity**.

BECOMING A PEAK PERFORMER

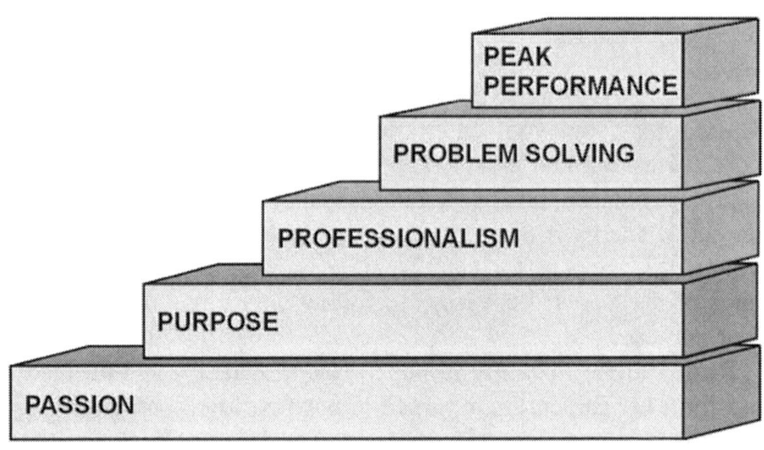

THE PEAK PERFORMANCE HEALTH CHECK

How can you continue to deliver peak performances? Great performers often follow their passion, translate this into a clear purpose; do professional work; find positive solutions to challenges and deliver peak performances. This exercise invites you to rate yourself in these areas – then clarify ways you can keep improving.

The activity in which I want to become a Class Act is:

- ______________________________

PASSION – The extent to which I am following my passion when doing this activity is:

_____/10

The steps I can take to make sure I am following my passion and thereby improve the rating are:

- to ______________________________
- to ______________________________
- to ______________________________

PURPOSE – The extent to which I have a clear purpose when doing this activity is:

_____/10

The steps I can take to make sure I have a clear purpose and thereby improve the rating are:

- to ______________________________
- to ______________________________
- to ______________________________

PROFESSIONALISM – The extent to which am I behave in a professional way when doing this activity is:

_____/10

The steps I can take to improve my professionalism and thereby improve the rating are:

- to ______________________________
- to ______________________________
- to ______________________________

PROBLEM SOLVING – The extent to which I find positive solutions to challenges when doing this activity is:

_____/10

The steps I can take to develop my ability to find positive solutions and thereby improve the rating are:

- to ______________________________
- to ______________________________
- to ______________________________

PEAK PERFORMANCE – The extent to which I produce peak performance – consistently delivering at least 8/10 – when doing this activity is:

_____/10

The steps I can take to deliver peak performance more consistently and thereby improve the rating are:

- to ______________________________
- to ______________________________
- to ______________________________

CONSISTENCY: MY ACTION PLAN

The steps I can take to continue developing the consistency required to succeed in my chosen activity are:

1. to ____

____

2. to ____

____

3. to ____

____

4. to ____

____

CREATIVITY

Introduction

Class Acts employ the right creativity at the right time to get the right results. Creativity comes in different forms, but three themes underlie most approaches. Great performers have the Radar and Repertoire required to deliver Results. What does this mean? First, they have great 'radar' in their chosen field. Employing their 'sixth sense,' they quickly see patterns and the potential picture of perfection. They then extrapolate these patterns and anticipate possible scenarios. Second, they have the repertoire – the strengths, strategies and skills – required to capitalize on what they see with their radar. Third, they apply their radar and repertoire to deliver results. Age brings experience and, hopefully, wisdom. Class Acts employ this knowledge to make creative breakthroughs when it matters.

Let's revisit the score you gave yourself regarding creativity. How did you rate on a scale of 0 to 10? What were the reasons you gave this score? Looking at your chosen activity, what kinds of creativity must somebody demonstrate to be successful? Which qualities do you have? Which can you improve? Let's consider how to boost your score.

You can develop your personal radar

Al Siebert, author of *The Survivor Personality*, coined the term 'personal radar.' Peak performers are good at seeing patterns, he said, in their specific area of expertise. Scanning the situation quickly to gather information, they extrapolate these patterns and envisage potential scenarios. They then choose their course of action. Ellen MacArther, the round-the-world yachtswoman, for example, reads the waves to anticipate sailing conditions. She then works out her future strategy. Gifted people follow a similar process in their chosen field, be they retailers, builders, carpenters, artists, athletes, dancers or whatever. They appear 'to know what will happen before it happens.' Entering their element, they perceive three things with their radar.

1. They see the successful and the self-defeating patterns.
2. They see the potential picture of perfection.
3. They see how to build on the successful patterns, and eliminate the self-defeating ones, to achieve the picture of perfection.

Where do you quickly see patterns? This is the key to where you have good radar. You may have a 'feeling' for a particular field – be it retailing, engineering, computing, people management, painting, architecture or whatever. Try tackling the exercise on this theme called *Pattern Recognition*.

What about other clues? When entering the situation in which you have good radar, you suddenly become alert. Employing your 'antennae,' you go 'A, B … Z.' You cannot understand why other people do not see the 'obvious.' Starting from the destination, you act quickly and reach it successfully. Tackle the exercise on this theme called *Personal Radar*. First, describe the specific activity in which you have good radar. Second, describe what indicates that you have this ability. Third, describe how you can capitalize on this gift. For example, how can you put yourself in more situations where you see patterns quickly?

CREATIVITY

The activity in which I want to become a Class Act is:

- ______________________________

The kinds of creativity I believe some one must demonstrate to be a Class Act in this activity are:

- to ______________________________
- to ______________________________
- to ______________________________

The kinds of creativity I already have are:

- to ______________________________
- to ______________________________
- to ______________________________

The kinds of creativity I need to add or improve are:

- to ______________________________
- to ______________________________
- to ______________________________

CLASS ACTS HAVE PERSONAL RADAR

Class Acts use their personal radar and professional repertoire to get positive results.

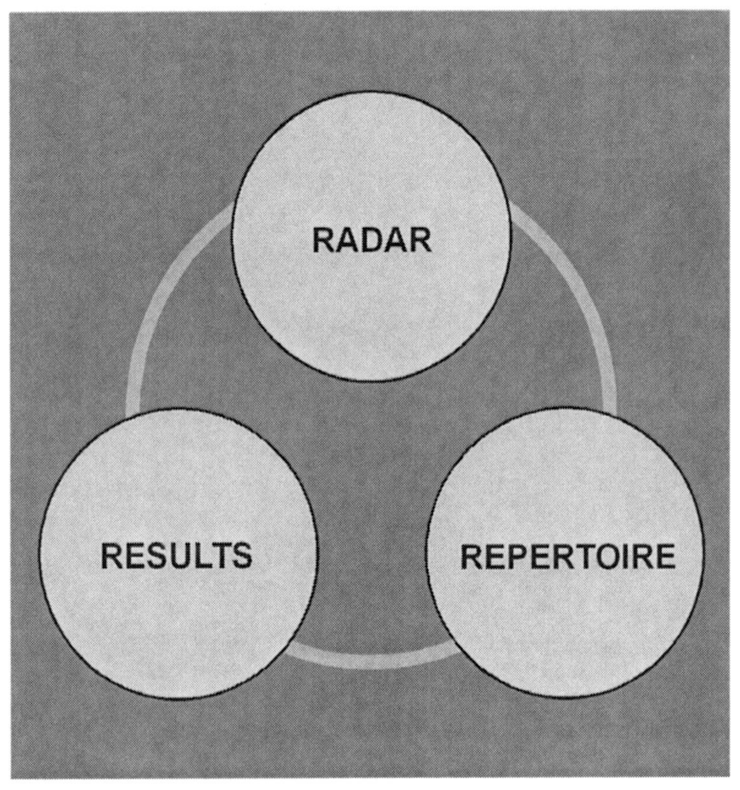

PATTERN RECOGNITION

Pattern recognition is one of the keys to personal radar. This exercise invites you to focus on where you have this ability.

The situations in which I rapidly see patterns are:

1) When I am ________________________________

The kinds of patterns I see are:

- ________________________________
- ________________________________
- ________________________________

2) When I am ________________________________

The kinds of patterns I see are:

- ________________________________
- ________________________________
- ________________________________

PERSONAL RADAR

The specific activity in which I have goods radar is:

- ____________________

The specific things that tell me I have good radar in this activity are:

- ____________________
- ____________________
- ____________________
- ____________________

The steps I can take to put myself in more situations where I have good radar are:

- ____________________
- ____________________
- ____________________
- ____________________

Great educators are fine talent spotters. One of the tools they use is to spot where people have good radar. Twenty years ago, I had the opportunity to practice this approach when working as a Youth Development Officer for a Swedish soccer club. Star players from around the county came for trials. My role was to select the best and mould them into a team. The players' skill levels were already high, so we watched where each individual thought strategically and 'took pictures of the play.' Taking this helicopter view increased their ability to influence a match.

> Lars, a 15 year old, began his first practice game poorly. One year younger than the other boys, he seemed out of his depth. Playing on the right wing, he hardly touched the ball and shrank into his shell. Speaking with our scouts at half-time, they said his best role was as a central defender. Switching Lars to that position, he became calmer, read the game well and commanded the defense. Two years later he became the under-19 captain. So why had he played on the wing? *'My previous coach said I must improve my weaknesses, so he put me on the wing,'* said Lars. *'I still played well against boys of my own age - which is why I got the trial, but had problems against older defenders. It felt good to go back to my natural position.'* My coaching role often involved switching players around to find where they had good radar. Feeling at home in a position, they would suddenly have 'lots of time.' They thought strategically and used their skills to achieve success.

When do you have 'lots of time'? When do things go 'slowly yet speedily'? When do you think strategically? Putting yourself in these situations increases the likelihood of performing great work. But it is only part of the story. Let's move onto the next step.

You can develop your professional repertoire

Radar provides you with lots of information: but how can you use it? Class Acts then dip into their professional repertoire and select the right tools to achieve success. Ellen MacArthur draws on her natural talent and hard-earned knowledge to guide the yacht through the storms. Raymond Blanc uses his ability to combine tasty ingredients to present a stunning meal. Steven Speilberg employs many different cinematic techniques when creating blockbuster films. Three main components make up your professional repertoire.

- First – **Strengths** – the natural gifts you have been given.
- Second – **Strategies** – the life experience and models you have gathered.
- Third – **Skills** – the skills you have mastered. How does this work in practice?

Let's imagine you are an educator who has been asked to run a workshop for managers. Regardless of what subject you are teaching, you will have a wide repertoire for helping people to learn. Great educators, for example, often follow the 3 Is: **Inspiration, Implementation** and **Integration**. They (a) create an inspiring environment, (b) offer implementation tools that work and (c) help people to integrate the learning into their daily lives. Designing the workshop, you will employ your radar and repertoire to answer the following questions around the 3 Is.

• INSPIRATION

How can I create an inspiring environment? How can I make sure I give the learners what they want? Who are the actual people who will be coming to the workshop? What are the key challenges they face? What will they want to 'take away' from the workshop? What, for them, will make it a successful session? What are the actual words I want people to be saying when they leave the session? For example: 'That was enjoyable. I got lots of practical tools. Now I know how to lead my people successfully.' How can I do my best to make sure they are saying these words? Bearing these answers in mind, what will be the three key goals of the workshop?

Finalizing the framework for the workshop, what will be the first theme, second theme, third theme, and so on? How can I bring each theme to life by following the '1-2-3' model for education: (1)

introduce the theme, (2) give an exercise on the theme and (3) sum-up the theme – then link to the next theme? How can I make the learning enjoyable and effective? How can I make it personal, practical and profitable? How can I make the learning materials user-friendly and attractive?

Returning to the actual first session of the workshop, how can I make people feel welcome? How can I give a good introduction? How can I set the right tone? How can I make the session professional but informal? How can I communicate the goals for the session? How can I double-check their agenda and make sure we are agreed on the goals? How can I make clear contracts about (a) my responsibility in the workshop and (b) the participants' responsibility? How can I get people to introduce themselves? How can I then grab people's attention and embark on the first theme? How can I make the learning exciting?'

• IMPLEMENTATION

Looking at each theme, how can I bring it to life? How can I pass on implementation tools that work? How can I give concrete examples that people will recognize? How can I use stories from work, business, sport and other aspects of life? How can I use different learning media? When can I offer direct input; provide models; do exercises; invite people to make presentations, etc.? How can I do everything possible to make the learning real, relevant and rewarding? How can I provide practical tools they can then use in their daily work?'

• INTEGRATION

How can I give people the chance to integrate the learning? How can I give them 'timeouts' to clarify their 'takeaways'? How can I spend one-to-one time with people during the workshop? How can they apply the learning to specific situations they meet in their work? How can they mentally rehearse the situation? How can they increase the chances of success? How can I follow-up with people after the session? What else can I do to ensure people achieve their goals on the workshop?'

Dipping into your repertoire, you will answer these questions and apply different tools and techniques to design the workshop. The next challenge will be to run it successfully.

Let's return to the activity in which you want to become a Class Act. How can you expand your professional repertoire? Which strengths, strategies and skills do you have already? Which can you add? How can you make this happen? Try tackling the exercise on this theme called *Professional Repertoire.* Personal radar is 'given' – you have a natural feeling for a particular activity, but it increases with wisdom. The real area for growth, however, lies in expanding the tools in your repertoire. Great performers then take the next step – they translate the ideas into action.

You can achieve positive results

Class Acts employ their radar and repertoire to get the right results. *'Rising stars are full of tricks,'* said one soccer manager, who had a reputation for nurturing young talent in his club. *'But they must channel their gifts to reach the top. They must develop consistency; then apply their creativity to help the team. Players that make this leap can become super stars, rather than stars of the local pub team.'* Similar rules apply in many fields. Class Acts often use their gifts to achieve their own goals, but many also focus on helping other people to succeed. Let's look at one person who built a world-wide reputation by following this route.

> Sylvia Ashton-Warner was a remarkable teacher who worked with Maori children in New Zealand during the 1930s. Experts flocked to study her methods because she achieved outstanding results helping the children to learn to read and write. What was her secret? Sylvia believed in organic reading and writing. Learning must be real: it should start from a person's experience and relate to their world. Writing in her book *Teacher*, she stresses the need to balance such beliefs with hard work and discipline.

Calling the children to attention each morning by playing the first eight notes of Beethoven's Fifth Symphony, Sylvia asks the class to tackle their work.

She calls each child to her in turn. *'What word do you want today?'* she asks Gayle, the first child, who replies: *'House.'* Sylvia writes the word on a piece of cardboard. She then asks Gayle to trace the word with her finger and say it out loud. Gayle 'owns' the word, it comes from her guts. Sylvia makes sure that Gayle says the word, sees the word and feels it in her body. She gives Gayle the cardboard, asks her to keep her 'word' for the day and repeats the process with each child. When class finishes Sylvia collects all the words on the pieces of cardboard.

Next morning Sylvia starts class by tipping the cardboard words onto the floor. *'Find your word,'* she tells the children. Gayle leaps from the chair and rummages in the pile. *'House,'* she shouts, *'I have found my word.'* She learned it by heart. Children have two visions, an inner vision and an outer vision, says Sylvia, and it is the inner vision which burns brightest. Gayle grasps the word which she spoke from her inner vision. Sylvia asks each child to choose a partner, speak their words and hear their partner's words. While the children teach each other, she repeats the process of inviting each child to choose their word for today. They build up what Sylvia calls their Key Vocabulary.

PROFESSIONAL REPERTOIRE

The activity in which I want to become a Class Act is:

- ______________________________

The specific strengths, strategies and skills I have in my repertoire are:

- ______________ • ______________
- ______________ • ______________
- ______________ • ______________

The specific things I would like to add to my repertoire are:

- ______________ • ______________
- ______________ • ______________
- ______________ • ______________

The specific steps I can take to add these things to my repertoire are:

- ______________ • ______________
- ______________ • ______________
- ______________ • ______________

What happens if Gayle fails to find her word? Sylvia rips up the piece of cardboard. The word has failed the 'one look' test and cannot have any great meaning for Gayle. Classrooms often display Jack and Jill illustrations for introducing the reading vocabulary to five-year-olds, says Sylvia, but it is a vocabulary chosen by educationalists in Auckland. Gayle owns only those words that have come from deep within herself. She is more likely to love these words and want to write them on paper.

Sylvia helps the children to write by inviting them to draw pictures and add their own captions. They build up their words into sentences and create books about their experiences. Children write one word, then two sentences, then three, until six-year-olds are writing half a page a day and seven-year-olds a page or more a day. Sylvia continues:

'The drama of these writings could never be captured in a bought book. It could never be achieved in the most faithfully prepared teaching books. No one book could ever hold the variety of subjects that appears collectively in the infant room each morning. Moreover, it is written in the language that they use themselves. The books they write are the most dramatic and pathetic and colorful things I've ever seen on pages.'

Once they know the joy of creating their own words, says Sylvia, they reach out longingly to learn about other cultures. Reaching out for a book must become an organic action. She continues: *'Back to these first words. To these first books. They must be made out of the stuff of the child itself. For it is here, right in this first word, that the love of reading is born, and the longer this reading is organic the stronger it becomes, until by the time he arrives at the books of the new culture, he receives them as another joy rather than as a labor.'* Sylvia Ashton-Warner achieved success, so opponents found it hard to argue with her methods.

Class Acts select the right strategy at the right time to achieve success. Creativity calls for getting the right balance between 'opening up' and then 'closing down.' *'I have problems finishing things,'* said one person. *'Over the last five years I have been trying to complete a book. Writing the first 50 pages is fine, but then I read other people's books and want to include many new ideas, so my book never gets finished.'* How can you apply your creativity? Faced by a challenge, you will begin by gathering lots of information. Clarifying the picture of perfection, you will push many buttons to see what works. Committing to your chosen strategy, you will then implement it successfully. You will have gone through the process of employing your personal radar and professional repertoire to deliver positive results.

Looking back on this section: Where do you quickly see patterns? How can you put yourself in these situations? How can you improve your radar? How can you expand your repertoire? How can you apply your life-experience and imagination to find creative solutions to challenges? Conclude this section by completing the exercise on *Creativity: My Action Plan*. Then we can move onto the final step towards performing memorable work – adding that touch of **Class**.

CREATIVITY: MY ACTION PLAN

The steps I can take to apply the right creativity at the right time to get the right results are:

- to ____________________

____

____

- to ____________________

____

____

- to ____________________

____

____

CLASS

Introduction

Class Acts produce that 'touch of class' at special moments. The athlete demonstrates 'grace under pressure'; the soldier behaves courageously under fire; the mediator finds a last minute 'win-win solution; the 'victor' behaves generously; the 'loser' makes a gracious speech. There are three kinds of special moments – (a) the 'creative' moment, when you are pursuing an activity and experience an epiphany, (b) the 'cherry on the cake' moment, when you have completed a task successfully and add that 'little bit extra,' and (c) the 'critical' moment, when you perform brilliantly under pressure. Many people live for those moments — because it is when they feel fully alive.

Great performers become very calm at such moments. Things seem to go 'slowly but speedily.' They then 'climb the mountain at the top of the mountain' by taking five steps towards reaching the summit.

1. **Clarity** – they establish the real results to achieve.
2. **Creativity** – they quickly explore all the 'conventional' and 'creative' options.
3. **Commitment** – they commit themselves to their chosen route.
4. **Concrete Results** – they deliver the goods.
5. **Class** – they often reach their goal by demonstrating that touch of class.

How do they make magic? Great performers become selfless at such moments. Putting themselves in the background, they relax, re-centre and refocus. They then flow, focus and finish. Sometimes they produce 'something special.' Sometimes the solution seems stunningly simple, but therein lies its genius. Sounds a long process, but Class Acts can go through the stages in a split second.

Let's revisit the score you gave yourself regarding class. How did you rate on a scale of 0 to 10? What is the reason you gave this score? Looking at your chosen activity, what qualities do you believe somebody must have to demonstrate that touch of class? Which do you have already? Which can you improve? Let's explore how you can boost your score.

You can look ahead to a potential special moment

Looking into the future, pick a time when you want to show that 'touch of class.' Peak performers continually anticipate potential scenarios. Arie de Guis, the author of *The Living Organism*, said such people develop a 'memory of the future.' They rehearse tackling challenges such as making tough decisions, solving conflicts or putting on the 18th green to win the Ryder Cup. Suddenly they find themselves in the moment and say: 'Now I feel alive. This is what life is about.' Staying calm, they clarify the picture of perfection. Staying positive, they 'focus on the top, rather than the drop.' When do you want to grace under pressure? Perhaps it is when confronting a challenge in your professional life – with a colleague or customer. Perhaps it is a challenge in your personal life – with a child or partner. Perhaps it is a time when you want to stay calm – but find it difficult. Describe the specific situation that you would later like to be able to look back on with pride.

The specific situation in which I would like to demonstrate a touch of class is:

- when ______________________________

____

Class Acts 'climb the mountain at the top of the mountain'

They focus on:

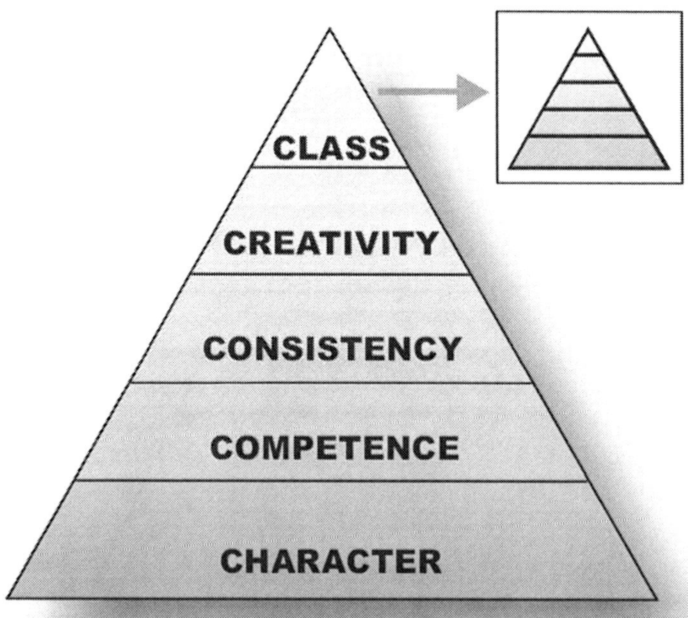

Choose an activity in which you can become a Class Act

Climbing the mountain at the top of the mountain

Class Acts focus on:

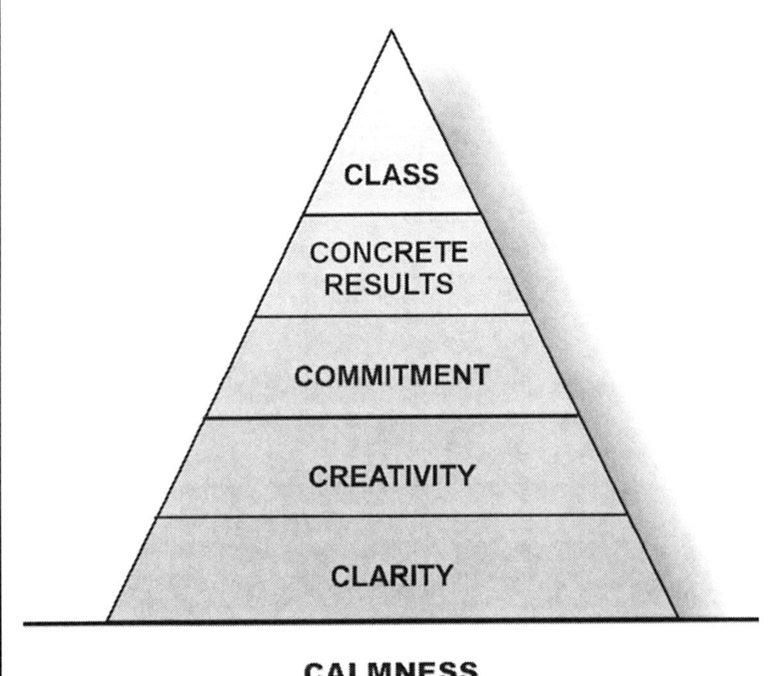

CLASS

The activity in which I want to become a Class Act is:

- ______________________________

The touches of class somebody must demonstrate to be a Class Act in this activity are:

- to ______________________________
- to ______________________________
- to ______________________________

The touches of class I already have are:

- to ______________________________
- to ______________________________
- to ______________________________

The touches of class I need to add or improve are:

- to ______________________________
- to ______________________________
- to ______________________________

You can focus on calmness

How do you normally behave in such moments – especially when you feel under pressure? Class Acts go into the 'C Zone': they become calm, controlled and centered. Faced by a difficult challenge, they empty themselves of feeling and become almost detached. Why? Otherwise they are overcome by emotion and become paralyzed. The negotiator remains cool on the rocky road towards freeing hostages – even when faced by a last minute hitch. The doctor arriving at a motorway accident 'hovers' above the carnage to get the big picture. Michael Jordan, the former basketball star, was like many outstanding athletes – he seemed to have more time than opponents. He stayed calm when his team were trailing 79-81 with just 10 seconds left on the clock. Regaining the ball, he called a 'Time Out' and gathered his team mates to agree on their game plan. Great performers remain still at the heart of the storm.

Looking back on your life, have you ever experienced such calmness? Maybe you faced a professional crisis. Maybe it was a personal crisis. Maybe everything around you seemed to be collapsing: but you took charge and solve the problem successfully. What did you do right then? Try tackling the exercise on this theme called *Calmness*. How did you 'buy time'? Many people have a 'ritual for re-centering' at such moments. They relax, re-center and refocus.

Do you have a 'ritual for re-centering'? *'Sometimes if I argue with my partner, I go out for a walk.'* said one person. *'Slowing down and appreciating nature puts everything into perspective. Returning to the house, both of us seem calmer.' 'Sometimes I get frustrated in meetings,'* said another person. *'In the old days I lashed out at colleagues, gaining a reputation for being arrogant and dismissive. Now I ration myself to three fights a year. I say to myself 'stay calm,' bite my lip and write notes on my pad – frequently planning what to do after the meeting. Now I concentrate on running my own department, rather than criticizing other manager's performances.'*

Looking ahead to the potential special moment, describe:

The specific things I can do to stay calm in the situation are:

- to ______________________________

- to ______________________________

- to ______________________________

You can focus on clarity

Class Acts experience remarkable clarity at special moments by asking themselves: 'What are the real results I want to achieve?' Sounds obvious, but it is not always easy. Imagine three separate scenarios.

1. You are leading an Everest team about to embark on the final ascent to the summit. Is your aim (a) to reach the summit, (b) to ensure the climbers get back safely or (c) to do both?
2. You are the Sales Director for a company and believe in providing customized solutions that help the customer to succeed. Suddenly you discover that a troublesome team member has not prepared properly for the vital customer presentation tomorrow. Is your aim (a) to motivate the unmotivated person, (b) to produce a great presentation that will lead to getting more business or (c) to avoid such problems in the future by employing real professionals?
3. You are arguing with your partner at home. Is your aim (a) to win the argument, (b) to build a long term 'win-win' relationship in which both people grow?

Faced with making a crucial decision, Class Acts focus on their picture of perfection.

> Michael Jordan recognized that, with 10 seconds left, his basketball team must clarify their specific goal. Trailing 79-81, they could aim (a)

> to shoot from within the 'D' and score a 2 point basket to level the scores, (b) to shoot from outside the 'D' and get a 3 point basket to win the game. Which should they attempt? They decided (a) to go for the 3 pointer, but (b) to shoot with just three seconds left which, should they miss, provided the insurance policy of winning the rebound – then shooting to tie the game. (Scoring a 3 pointer too early would give opponents time to break away and retake the lead.) Michael Jordan's team was then ready to create their strategy.

Looking back in your life: Can you remember a critical time when you experienced remarkable clarity? Did you start from the destination – the real results to achieve – and then work backwards? 'Sounds logical, but sometimes you have several targets – or even contradictory aims,' somebody may say. 'How do you clarify your real goals?' Class Acts brainstorm all the results they want to achieve – then list these in order of priority. They may also make short-, medium- and long-term plans. Looking ahead to your potential special moment, describe:

The real results I want to achieve in the situation are:

- to ____

- to ____

- to ____

CALMNESS

This exercise invites you to do three things. First, describe a specific time when you demonstrated calmness in a difficult situation. Second, describe what you did right to ensure you were calm – and maybe helped others to be calm. Third, describe what you can do to demonstrate calmness when faced by possible difficult situations in the future.

The specific time I demonstrated calmness was:

- when I ____________________

The specific things I did right to be calm then were:

- I ____________________
- I ____________________
- I ____________________

The specific things I can do to stay calm in the future – especially in tough situations – are:

- I can ____________________
- I can ____________________
- I can ____________________

You can focus on creativity

Class Acts clarify the 'What' – then move onto the 'How.' Scanning multiple options simultaneously, they explore (a) the 'conventional solutions' – the obvious ones and (b) the 'creative solutions.' Considering each option in turn, they then outline the consequences. Exploring their repertoire, they select the strategy most likely to achieve success. (People who are dyslexic – or others who have overcome adversity – often make great problem-solvers. Early on in life, they learned to employ multiple strategies. Suffering at old-fashioned schools, such people often blossomed later in roles that required lateral thinking.)

Imagine you are a Sales Director who faces a tough challenge. Tomorrow Ken, the difficult team member, must make a crucial presentation to a key customer. Out of the blue, you discover he hasn't prepared properly. Blustering his way through your questions, Ken maintains he can 'wing it.' How to find a solution? You quickly prioritize the results to achieve, which are (1) to provide solutions that help the customer to succeed, (2) to make a great presentation – plus possibly employing other strategies – to get more business, and (3) to avoid similar situations in the future. So what are your options? There are several possibilities.

(a) Ignore the problem and hope for the best (not an attractive option).

(b) Harangue and supervise Ken into making a good presentation.

(c) Coach Ken – which will entail making a clear coaching contract. You can start by agreeing with Ken on the picture of perfection. For example, 'The actual words we want the customer to be saying after the presentation are … …' Ken can describe how he can ensure the customers say these things, plus the help he wants from you as a coach. You and he can then work together to achieve the goals.

(d) Take an immediate 'hands-on role' and make the presentation yourself. This may mean standing in as the customer Account Director for the next three months. You can release Ken, or invite him to play a supporting role. The next step will be to form a new team to build a better relationship with the customer.

(e) Ring the customer and set up one-to-one meetings with key individuals tomorrow morning. You can explain it is vital to double-check that the afternoon presentation fully addresses their needs, and can include any new issues that may have arisen. (This will mean working late tonight to create the proposal, slide-deck and background notes.) Adopting this approach will also provide the opportunity to deepen customer relationships and increase the chances of future business.

(f) After the presentation, take the tough decisions required to ensure this problem never happens in the future. This calls for building a super team of true professionals.

Faced by such a challenge, you will quickly brainstorm the choices and consequences. Exploring each option in turn, you will ask yourself questions like: What are the pluses and minuses? How attractive is each option? What are the best parts of each route? Can I put these together to create another option? Are there any other imaginative solutions? You will then be in a position to commit to a particular strategy.

Michael Jordan's basketball team followed a similar process – starting by agreeing on the 'What.' They aimed to get 3 points – but also had a back up plan for capitalizing on any rebound and scoring 2 points. 'How' to make this happen? Starting from the desired result, they ask: Who wants to throw the deciding shot? Where should they shoot from on the court? Who should be positioned to pick up any rebound? Bearing these aims in mind, how can we score the 3 points? What is our strategy? Reviewing the set moves practiced in training, they consider the straightforward options, before exploring the potential variations. Surveying their repertoire of options, they select the most promising strategy.

How do you find creative solutions? Looking back in your life, can you recall a time when you tackled a problem and quickly surveyed the different options? How did you generate all the possibilities? How did you evaluate the consequences? How can you follow similar principles in the future? Looking ahead to your potential special moment, describe:

The possible creative solutions in this situation are:

- to ____

- to ____

- to ____

You can focus on commitment

Class Acts commit themselves to implementing their chosen strategy. They then make a concrete action plan. (Sometimes they choose to pursue parallel strategies simultaneously.) Choosing and committing to a strategy sounds a long process, but sometimes only takes a split-second. Once committed to a course of action, you go for it 100%.

Imagine you are the Sales Director who discovered that Ken planned to 'wing it' at the customer presentation. How can you do your best (a) for the customer; (b) for your company, (c) for your colleagues, (d) for ensuring this problem never occurs in the future and (e) for Ken? You decide to take over as the Account Director and make tomorrow's presentation. The first step is to meet Ken and explain your decision. Accepting he may not agree with your conclusions, you outline the options, then explain your chosen route. Ken can contribute to the presentation, but you will set the ground rules. Concluding the conversation, you then ring the customer to set up one-to-one meetings. Tonight you will prepare the proposal and presentation. Tomorrow you will listen to the customer and find 'win-win' solutions. The following day you will take the tough decisions required to build a professional team.

> Michael Jordan's team also committed to their chosen strategy. They agreed their game plan for taking the 3-point shot with three seconds left on the clock. Teamwork calls for clarity, contracting and concrete results. Everybody must be crystal clear on (a) what mountain they are climbing – the specific goals, (b) how they are climbing it – the strategy, and (c) who will be doing What and When – the specific action plan. Michael Jordan's team knew who must move where and when, and who must take the final shot. Breaking from their huddle, they took up their respective positions on the court.

Reflecting on your life, can you remember a critical time when you committed yourself to a particular strategy? Did you consider the different options? Did you explore the consequences? Did you find creative solutions? Did you make a conscious choice about the route you wanted to pursue? Did you make a specific action plan? Did you have a backup strategy? If other people were involved, did you make clear contracts? Did you then commit yourself 100%? Can you follow similar principles in the future in your personal or professional life? Looking at your potential special moment, describe:

The specific things I can do to commit myself to my chosen strategy in the situation are:

- to ____

- to ____

- to ____

You can focus on concrete results

Class Acts deliver the goods at crucial moments. They lead mountaineers safely back to base camp; make a stunning customer presentation; solve conflicts by creating 'win-win' solutions. Realizing they can only 'control the controllables,' they concentrate on doing their best to reach the goals. Putting on the 18th green to win the Ryder Cup, for example, the golfer reminds himself to 'play the shot, not the occasion.' Peak performers increase the odds, however, by taking the following steps.

- **They start by refocusing on the picture of perfection.**

Taking a final look at the 'summit,' they pause for a moment to reflect. Focusing on 'the top rather than the drop,' they embrace a positive attitude and rehearse their chosen strategy. Giving themselves a final reminder to work hard, they then step towards reaching their goal.

- **They focus on the process as much as the prize**

'Staying in the moment,' they do the right things in the right way to get the right results. Putting to win the Ryder Cup, for example, you concentrate on the process rather than the prize. Placing yourself in a 'cocoon of concentration,' you concentrate on striking the ball, rather than declaring victory – or defeat – too early. Peak performers have great attention to detail, especially at critical moments. They recognize that giving 100% to the task is the only way to succeed.

- **They perform brilliantly when it matters and do their best to achieve the picture of perfection**

Class Acts have often 'been there before.' They know what to expect in the heat of battle – so the feelings they experience do not come as a surprise. Previously they may have become paralyzed when entering this territory. Learning from setbacks and successes, they have developed resilience. Magical artistry may be required, but it must contribute to reaching the goals – not act as a replacement. Michael Jordan's team contained many star players, but they combined their talents, rather than working alone on the basketball court. They played hard to implement the strategy and score the points. Great finishers do everything possible to reach their goals.

Peak performers focus on the process as much as the prize

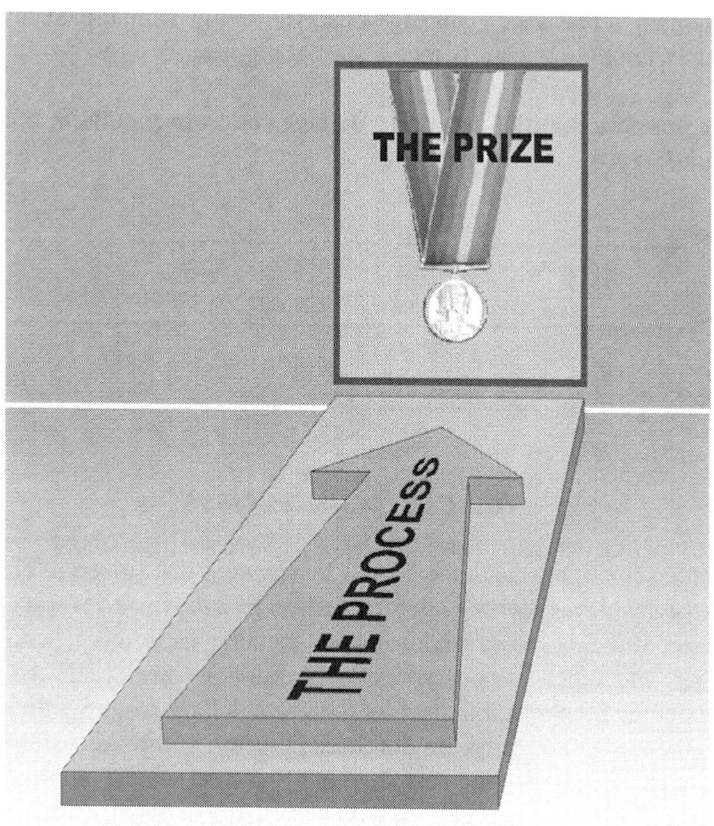

Class Acts also see things in perspective. Some events are a matter of life or death – but most are not. 'Success' may be sweet, but can be temporary. Winning a sports championship or a business deal may be uplifting, but pales against the joy of having a healthy child. Wise people know what really matters. Paradoxically, this ability to see things in perspective, and not try to grasp the results, increases the chances of 'success.'

Looking back on your life, can you recall a time when you sweated hard to deliver concrete results? Did you take a final look at the picture of perfection? Did you focus on the process as much as the prize? Did you do everything possible to achieve the results? What did you do right then to reach the goals? How can you follow similar paths in the future? Looking at your potential special moment, describe:

The specific things I can do to deliver concrete results in the situation are:

- to ____________________

- to ____________________

- to ____________________

You can focus on class

People sometimes reach their goals by showing that 'touch of class.' The rugby player scores a last minute drop goal to win the World Cup; Nelson Mandela shows kindness when meeting his former jailers; the singer concludes a concert by performing a memorable encore without the orchestra; Michael Jordan scores a long-range 3 pointer to win the basketball game. As the Sales Director, you make a stunning presentation, listen to the customer and find 'win-win' solutions. You will do everything possible to help the customer to succeed – then find some way to add that touch of class.

Different people show class in different ways. Sometimes they produce 'something special.' Sometimes they produce a solution that seems stunningly simple. How do people produce such magic? The theory is simple. Going into their equivalent of the 'zone,' things seem to go 'slowly yet speedily.' They relax, re-centre and refocus – then flow, focus and finish. Putting themselves in the background, they become selfless and use their strengths to achieve their picture of 'success.'

Some people show class as human beings. Imagine you are a Polish Catholic mother in 1942. Suddenly a 12-year-old Jewish boy knocks on your door. He is running from the Nazis, who have killed his family. Hungry and frightened, he has nowhere to hide. What would you do? Would your response be (a) to close the door, (b) to tell the authorities or (c) to take him into your home? Samuel Oliner, author of *Do Unto Others: Extraordinary Acts Of Ordinary People*, describes how he – the 12-year-old boy – was saved by Bulwina, the Polish mother. Protecting him from the Nazis, she spelled out her instructions. He must change his name to Jusek; go to church every Sunday; learn the Catholic Catechism; get a job and make sure nobody saw him if he undressed. Balwina protected him for a while, but then the situation became too dangerous. He trekked across the country with other refugees.

Samuel Oliner escaped, traveled to America and, with Pearl Oliner, eventually wrote *The Altruistic Personality*. That book chronicles the activities of 'rescuers.' Some 500,000 non-Jews risked their own lives to rescue the victims of Nazi persecution. They were 'ordinary' people: farmers, teachers, entrepreneurs, factory workers, rich and poor, Protestants and Catholic. Different people helped the Jews in different ways. Some offered them shelter; some helped them escape from prison; some smuggled them out of the country. The rescuers showed that people can do wonderful things, even in the midst of catastrophe. Why? Some rescuers had close connections with Jews before the War; others had strong moral beliefs and translated their love into action. One Italian gives a typical answer to the question that is often asked of rescuers: 'How could you be so courageous?'

'It was all something very simple. Nothing grandiose was done. It was done simply without considering risk, without thinking about

whether it would be an occasion for recognition or to be maligned. It was, in effect, done out of innocence. I didn't think I was doing anything other that what should be done, or that I was in any special danger because of what I was doing. Justice had to be done. Persecution of the innocents was unacceptable.'

'It was the natural thing to do. I did not think about it,' is the answer given by other people who show courage. For example, a soldier rescuing a fallen comrade or a passer-by pulling an injured driver from a car. Samuel Oliner's research showed, however, that the rescuer's actions stemmed from strong moral values. Considering their options, even if only for a split second, they chose to be true to themselves, rather than live with the memory of betraying their values. Choosing to live in what the Existentialists called 'Good Faith,' rather than 'Bad Faith,' they demonstrated class as human beings.

Many individuals show touches of class every day. People who are Encouragers, for example, love to help others to succeed. Generous hearted, they prefer to give rather than receive. *'I get an almost permanent high from encouraging people,'* said one educator. *'Every day I pass on knowledge to my students, which is incredibly fulfilling.'* So what happens when people enter that dimension where they do such remarkable work? Settling on their specific goals, they focus on three things.

a. They become *selfless*

'You are most yourself when you forget yourself,' we are told. Putting themselves in the background, people speak about 'surrendering to a process – almost a higher force.' Athletes describe 'going into the zone.' Writers say 'the article wrote itself.' Great work often emerges from pursuing a sense of service. (Ego-driven people may never find fulfillment. Applause provides a temporary kick, but is soon replaced by the hunger for greater recognition.) Sages talk about life being a three stage process: 'Find yourself, accept yourself and then forget yourself. Serving others is the way to be your true self.'

b. They build-on their *strengths*

Class Acts employ their talents to achieve 'success.' Reaching into their soul, they define themselves as volunteers, rather than victims. 'Give it to me,' they say, 'I want to tackle the challenge. Afterwards I want to feel physically and psychologically exhausted. I cannot live with myself if I hold back.' Drawing upon hard-earned wisdom, they step into the arena to pursue their chosen strategy. Capitalizing on their radar, they reach into their repertoire and aim to achieve the picture of perfection.

c. They do everything possible to achieve *success*

'Success' means different things to different people. Individuals may define it as, for example, leaving a legacy, winning an Olympic Gold, finding a cure for AIDS, providing a great childhood for their children or laying down their life for others. Embracing the moment, Class Acts do whatever is necessary to reach the goal. People sometimes report entering an almost trance-like state. Only later can they recall what happened and clarify the learning. They then apply the wisdom to future special moments.

Looking back on your life, can you think of a time when you added that 'touch of class'? Perhaps it was during a 'creative moment' when you had a breakthrough epiphany; a 'cherry on the cake moment' when you had already completed a task, then added that little bit extra; or a 'critical' moment when you performed well under pressure. What did you do right then to deliver the goods? How can you follow similar principles in the future? Looking at your potential special moment, describe:

The specific things I can do to add that touch of class in the situation are:

- to ____

- to ____

- to ____

You can practice Class Act thinking

'Sounds fine in theory,' somebody may say. 'But what about the situations I find difficult? For example, arguing with my partner, firing an employee at work or holding my temper during boring meetings. Are there any techniques I can use to improve my behavior?'

Great performers continually practice mental rehearsal – especially when facing potentially critical moments. You can employ this approach by tackling the exercise called *Class Act Thinking*. First, describe a difficult problem you may encounter in your personal or professional life. Second, ask yourself: 'How would a class act behave in this situation?' This is the crucial question. Describe how you believe such a person would behave. Third, looking at the answers you have listed, describe how you follow these steps in your own way. Make an action plan. People often find that adopting this approach helps them to stay calm during crises.

Reflecting on the topics covered in this section, choose a crucial moment you may face in the future. Looking ahead, how can you stay calm? How can you establish clarity? How can you find creative solutions? How can you commit yourself to a strategy? How can you deliver concrete results? How can you add that touch of class?

Faced by a difficult challenge in your personal or professional life, how can you practice class act thinking? If you wish, consolidate your ideas in the exercise called **Class: My Action Plan**. After that, let's move onto the final step.

CLASS ACT THINKING

What would a Class Act do in this situation?

This exercise invites you to focus on what, for you, may be difficult situations. First, describe a potentially difficult problem you may face in the future. Second, ask yourself: 'How would a class act behave in this situation?' Describe what you believe they would do. Third, describe how you can follow these steps in your own way.

The potentially difficult situation is:

- ______________________________

The things I would do in this situation are:

- to ______________________________
- to ______________________________
- to ______________________________

The things I can therefore do to behave like a Class Act in this situation are:

- to ______________________________
- to ______________________________
- to ______________________________

CLASS: MY ACTION PLAN

The steps I can take to add the 'Touch of Class' required to succeed in my chosen activity are:

1. to ______________________________

____

____

2. to ______________________________

____

____

3. to ______________________________

____

____

Conclusion — Creating the place to be a Class Act

'Recognizing my top talent is the "What",' somebody may say, *'but "How" can I put it into practice? My present role is okay – but the fulfillment factor is only 6/10. Promotion is a possibility, but I will get bored in meetings. Five years ago, I entered the Faustian Pact. I planned to work hard for five years, make money and then be free to do what I wanted. Unfortunately it has become a rolling five years. Paradoxically, the more status I get, the less time I spend doing what I enjoy. The time has come to return to work that gives me a buzz: but where can I do what I do best? Have you any suggestions?'*

People want three things from work: money, meaning and magic. Money feeds the stomach, but meaning and magic feed the spirit and the soul. How can you balance your finances and fulfillment? How can you create the opportunity to be a Class Act? Three main routes stand out. You can focus on your present role, craft a potential role or generate possible new audiences. Let's explore these roads.

• Present role

You can try to use your 'A' talent more often in your present role. Sounds attractive but, unless you are already in your perfect role, the chances are around 2/10. Why?

There are two reasons. First, roles are often 'historical' and were designed 'to win the last war.' Today's fast moving world, however, calls for finding new ways to satisfy customers. Great organizations focus on the results to achieve and continually redesign the roles to deliver these results. Dying organizations stick to the old format and old roles. Second, roles consist of many 'givens.' Countless tasks are handed down to complete, but these may not match your talents. How to tell if you are in the right niche? Looking at your present role, ask yourself the following question. 'Bearing in mind my strengths, what percentage of my time is devoted to doing what I do best?' The minimum figure you are looking for is at least 50%. You may then have the basis for expanding the role into one that is fulfilling. If not, you may wish to look for a more appropriate fit. Let's explore the second route.

• Potential role

You can craft a potential role that is a 'Win-Win' for both you and an employer. Providing you have enlightened employers, the chances are around 6/10. The key is convincing potential sponsors. How to make this happen? Decision-makers always want to improve their profitability, product quality and people. Show how what you can offer will improve any or all of these factors. Focus on the 'results,' rather than the role. One tip – do not go with an 'idea' – go with your first three customers. *'My manager was encouraging,'* said one person, *'but explained that I was too valuable in my present role. Moving me was too risky. So we agreed a contract to find and coach my successor. The recruitment process took three months, but eventually I moved to a role I found more fulfilling.'* People buy benefits, so show how crafting a new contribution will improve the business. Sometimes this approach works, sometimes you may move onto the third route.

• Possible new audiences

You can find or generate new audiences that will pay you for being a Class Act. This is the route taken by many pioneers in business, the arts, sports and other fields. The chances of success are 7+/10. This new audience may be inside or outside your present organization.

How to create such opportunities? Continually reach out to potential sponsors and help them to succeed. Let's return to the earlier exercise called *My Possible Niche*. Focus on the stimulation factor. What kind of project will be stimulating? What kind of people –

colleagues or customers – will be stimulating? What kind of place – culture and environment – will be stimulating? With these factors in mind, what might be your possible niche? What can you offer to potential sponsors? What challenges do they face? How can you help them to reach their goals? People buy people, so most work will come from your network. Real networking is about following the old-fashioned service ethic and helping others to succeed. Reach out to potential customers, keep planting seeds and somebody will eventually say: 'How can we take this further?' Sounds idealistic? Maybe – but it works.

People sometimes explore all three routes before creating a platform where they can be a Class Act. Imagine you are a backing singer in a West End musical, such as Chicago, but you want to earn a living singing soul classics. Certainly you can inject soul into your nightly role, but it may not be fully satisfying. You can approach the Director to show how doing a solo spot will be a 'win-win' and contribute to achieving the musical's goals. But ultimately you may need to generate an audience for your soul music. Performing in clubs on Sunday nights can build a following, sell records and eventually lead to your own show. Pioneers frequently take this third route – they find sponsors who will pay them for practicing their 'A' talent. Try tackling the exercise on this theme called *Class Act Possibilities*.

'Live, love, learn, labor and leave a legacy,' we are told. Everybody is an artist, everybody is creative. How can you develop your talent? How can you use your gifts to help other people? Try tackling the exercise called *Class Act Development Plan*. Describe the steps you can take to develop your **Character, Competence, Consistency, Creativity** and **Class**. Everybody suffers bruises and broken bones in their lives – but wise people use these experiences to enrich their legacy. They make a contribution that helps people and the planet. Take the ideas you like from this book and use them in your own way. Don't worry if you do not see instant results, because sometimes your flowers will grow tomorrow. Enjoy the journey towards becoming a Class Act.

CLASS ACT POSSIBILITIES

Creating the opportunities to be a Class Act

This exercise invites you to the opportunities to be a class act. Focus on three areas. (1) Present role – describe the steps you can take to use your top talent in your present role. (This may or may not be possible.) (2) Potential role – describe the steps you can take to craft a new role that will be a 'Win-Win' for both yourself and an employer. (3) Possible new audiences – describe the steps you can take to find or generate a new audience that will pay you for doing the activity in which you can be a class act. Bearing these options in mind, move onto an action plan. Describe the steps you can take to create the opportunities to be a class act.

The activity in which I want to become a Class Act is:

- ______________________________

PRESENT ROLE – The steps I can take to do more of these things in my present role are:

- to ______________________________
- to ______________________________
- to ______________________________

POTENTIAL ROLE – The steps I can take to craft a new role that is a 'win-win' for myself and an employer are:

- to ______________________________
- to ______________________________
- to ______________________________

POSSIBLE NEW AUDIENCES – The steps I can take to find or generate a new audience that will want what I offer as a Class Act are:

- to ______________________________
- to ______________________________
- to ______________________________

CLASS ACT POSSIBILITIES – Action Plan

Bearing in mind the possible options, the steps I can take to create the opportunities to be a Class Act are:

- to ______________________________
- to ______________________________
- to ______________________________

CLASS ACT DEVELOPMENT PLAN

This final exercise invites you to focus on how to continue improving in your chosen activity.

The activity in which I want to become a Class Act is:

- ______________________________

CHARACTER

The rating I give myself in terms of having the character to succeed in my chosen activity is: ______/10

The specific things I can do to improve this rating are:

- to ______________________________
- to ______________________________

COMPETENCE

The rating I give myself in terms of having the competence to succeed in my chosen activity is: ______/10

The specific things I can do to improve this rating are:

- to ______________________________
- to ______________________________

CONSISTENCY

The rating I give myself in terms of having the consistency to succeed in my chosen activity is: ______/10

The specific things I can do to improve this rating are:

- to ______________________________
- to ______________________________

CREATIVITY

The rating I give myself in terms of having the creativity to succeed in my chosen activity is: ______/10

The specific things I can do to improve this rating are:

- to ______________________________
- to ______________________________

CLASS

The rating I give myself in terms of having the class to succeed in my chosen activity is: ______/10

The specific things I can do to improve this rating are:

- to ______________________________
- to ______________________________

Appendices

Appendix 1

Class Act Coaching – Trigger Questions

Introduction

How can you continue to do great work? The following pages provide trigger questions that you can use to help yourself – or somebody else – to be a class act.

- Let's start by setting the scene. Who do you believe is a class act? Think of somebody who consistently performs brilliantly and then adds that touch of class – especially at crucial moments. This can be a person in sports, business, the arts or any field. What do they do right to perform great work? Let's move on to exploring where you can perform great work.

Choosing the activity in which you want to become a Class Act

- Can you think of a time when – even if only for a few moments – you behaved like a class act? Can you describe the situation? What did you do right then? How can you follow similar principles in the future?

- Let's move on to choosing the activity in which you feel you can become – and want to become – a class act. Choose one in which you experience three things: energy, ease and excellence. You get positive energy, feel at ease and get independent feedback that you excel. Let's consider these factors.

- What are the activities that give you energy? When do you live the 'A' life – feeling alive, rather than the 'B' life – feeling bored or the 'C' life – feeling cramped? When do you feel positively engaged, rather than partly engaged or pretend engaged? When do you feel excited? When do you get a 'creative fix'? When do you feel completely absorbed in an activity? When, for you, 'time goes away'? When do you experience a sense of flow? When do you experience your equivalent of going into the sporting 'zone'?

- Where do you feel at ease? Where do you feel in your element? When do you say: 'This is what I was meant to do'? What are the activities in which things 'come easily' for you? When do you quickly see patterns and the potential picture of perfection? When do you think strategically? What are the situations in which quickly see the desired destination? When do you go 'A, B … then leap to Z'? Who are the kind of people with whom you feel most at ease? What are their personality characteristics?

- When do you deliver excellence? When do you consistently produce As, rather than Bs or Cs? If you were a Managing Director, what would you hire yourself to deliver?

- Let's move on to exploring your positive history. Everybody has a preferred way of working, so let's find your successful style. Looking back at your life, describe the 'projects' that for you have been satisfying and successful. Considering each project in turn, describe what made it rewarding. Looking at these projects, can you see any patterns? If so, describe what you see as your successful style. Looking to the future, describe the kind of activity in which you will be able to follow your successful style. Looking at this potential activity, clarify to what extent you will deliver excellence. For example, do you score at least 8/10 on each of the 3 Ds – Drive, Detail and Delivery?

- Let's focus on three factors that will help you to clarify your possible niche.
    1. **Project** – describe the kind of 'project' you find stimulating.
    2. **People** – describe the kind of people you find stimulating –

both customers and colleagues.

3. **Place** – describe the 'place' – the culture and environment – you find stimulating. This may be a 'physical' a 'psychological' place.

Putting all these components together, describe the possible niche where you can do your best work.

- Move on to choosing the activity in which you want to become a class act. Dare to be super specific. The more specific you are, the more likely you are to be successful. How to be sure you have chosen the right niche? There are several checks worth doing.

1. How high does it score on **Energy, Ease** and **Excellence**?
2. Is it something you really care about? Check how high it scores on the **Caring Dimension**. You need to score at least 8/10 on caring about the outcome.
3. Is it an activity in which you can be a **Warrior-Wizard**? Do you enjoy the 80%+ warrior work – the grunt work? Can you also add the extra 20% wizard work – the great work? Make sure the niche is one in which you can be a Warrior-Wizard.

- Looking at your chosen activity: How high do you rate yourself in the areas of **Character, Competence, Consistency, Creativity** and adding that touch of **Class**? Mark yourself on a scale of 0 to 10. You may score at least 7/10 in each area – but remember it is an exponential climb from 7 to 10. Let's explore how you can improve the scores.

CHARACTER

- Let's revisit the score you gave yourself regarding character. How did you rate on a scale of 0 to 10? What is the reason you gave this score? What are the qualities you believe somebody must demonstrate to be successful in your chosen activity? Which qualities do you have already? Which do you need to develop?

Let's explore three aspects of character: **Drive, Discipline** and **Decision-making appetite**.

- **DRIVE**. How strong is your drive? Rate this on a scale of 0 to10. To what extent are you following your passion? Resilience is also crucial – so how do you manage setbacks? How long does it take you to bounce back? What is your strategy for dealing with difficulties?

- **DISCIPLINE**. Looking at your chosen activity, how strong is your discipline? Rate yourself on a scale of 0 to 10. Which disciplines do you believe are required to be successful? Which disciplines come to you naturally? Which can you improve? Which can you 'buy in' from elsewhere? When are your prime times – the times of the day when you have most energy? How can you capitalize on these prime times to increase your discipline?

- **DECISION MAKING APPETITE**. Looking at your chosen activity, to what extent do you relish making decisions – especially the tough ones? Rate yourself on a scale of 0 to 10. Describe three things. First, the decisions you do enjoy taking – including the tough ones. Second, the decisions you don't enjoy or find difficult. Third, the specific things you can do (a) to make more of the decisions you like taking and (b) to bolster your ability to take the tougher decisions. Let's move on to the next step.

COMPETENCE

- Let's revisit the score you gave yourself in terms of Competence. How did you rate yourself on a scale of 0 to 10? What is the reason you gave yourself this score? Let's consider three aspects of competence: **Strengths, Strategic decision-making ability** and **Skills**.

- **STRENGTHS**. Looking at your chosen activity, which strengths do you believe somebody must have to be successful? Which strengths do you have? How can you combine these strengths to produce something special? How can you employ these talents to reach your goals?

- **STRATEGIC DECISION MAKING**. How good are you at making strategic decisions? What is your model for making decisions? Looking at the Seven C Model, which parts come to you naturally? What can you improve in terms of **Calmness, Clarity, Choices, Consequences, Creative Solutions, Conclusions** and **Concrete Results**? Are there any specific areas in which you need to improve your strategic decision making?

- **SKILLS**. What are the skills somebody must demonstrate to be successful in your chosen field? Which skills do you have already? Which can you improve? Which can you 'buy in' from outside? How can you make this happen? Let's move onto the next step.

CONSISTENCY

- Let's revisit the score you gave yourself in terms of Consistency. Great workers always produce the goods. Overcoming setbacks and crises, they consistently deliver at least an 8/10. How do you rate yourself in terms of being consistent? What is the reason you gave yourself this score? Let's consider three aspects of consistency: being **Positive, Professional** and a **Peak Performer**.

- **POSITIVE**. On a scale of 0- to 10: To what extent do you have a positive attitude? How can you continue to develop this attitude? How can you control the controllables? Positive people put themselves in 'positive circles,' rather than 'negative circles.' How can you spend more time in positive relationships where you get a positive response and positive results? How can you avoid negative circles? How can you keep following good habits? What do you do well at the moment? How can you repeat these successful patterns? What can you do better and how?

- **PROFESSIONAL**. How high do you rate your professionalism in your chosen activity? Which aspects do you perform well? Which aspects can you improve? Proactivity is crucial: so how can you be more proactive, both with customers and colleagues? What are the issues that for you are now in the Green, Amber and Red Zones? How can you tackle these issues?

- **PEAK PERFORMANCE**. Looking at your chosen activity: Do you always score at least 8/10? How do you manage your physical, psychological and productive energy? Which parts do you manage well? Which can you manage better and how? How can you get the right balance between doing the great work and grunt work? Which parts of the grunt work do you want to keep? Which parts can you delegate, ditch or do in other ways?

- Finally in this section, let's do a peak performance health check. Great workers often focus on: (a) passion – they follow their passion; (b) purpose – they translate their passion into a clear purpose; (c) professionalism – they behave in a professional way; (d) problem-solving – they find solutions to problems; and (e) peak performance – they consistently deliver peak performances. How do you rate yourself in each of these areas? The first two stages are vital, because they provide the stimulation for doing great work. Are you still following your passion and translating this into a clear purpose? If not, how can you return to following your passion – even if in only a small way? Let's explore the next step.

CREATIVITY

- Success calls for employing the right creativity at the right time to get the right results. Bearing this in mind, what score did you give yourself on creativity? What is the reason you gave this score?

Creativity comes in different forms, but three themes underlie most approaches. Great performers have the **Radar** and **Repertoire** required to deliver **Results**. Let's explore these different aspects.

- **RADAR**. Where do you have good 'personal radar'? What are the situations in which you quickly see patterns? Where do you see pictures of perfection? When do you go: A, B … then leap to Z? What are the situations in which you seem to have 'lots of time'? Can you give an example? Are there particular kinds of people with whom you have good personal radar? Do they have certain characteristics? How can you put yourself in more situations where you have good radar?

- **REPERTOIRE**. You will get lots of information from your radar – but using it properly calls for having a wide repertoire. What are the **Strengths, Strategies** and **Skills** you have already in your repertoire? Which would you like to add? How can you expand your repertoire?

- **RESULTS**. Class Acts employ their personal radar and apply their professional repertoire to deliver positive results. How can you do this in your chosen activity? How can you get the right balance between 'opening up' – getting lots of information – and then 'closing down' to reach the goals? What can you do to produce positive results? Let's move onto the next step.

CLASS

- Let's revisit the score you gave yourself as showing class – especially at special moments. What is the reason you gave yourself this score? There are three kinds of special moments: (a) the 'creative' moment – when you are pursuing an activity and have an epiphany; (b) the 'cherry on the cake' moment – when you are already assured of success; and (c) the 'critical' moment – when you are under pressure. Which is the kind of moment in which you perform best?

Class Acts love to 'climb the mountain at the top of the mountain.' They start by being very calm. They then focus on **Clarity, Creative Solutions, Commitment, Concrete results** and **Class**. Can you recall a time when you went through some of these stages? Looking in the future: Can you think of a potential moment when you would like to show that touch of class? Describe the possible situation. Looking ahead to that time, let's explore the following steps.

- **CALMNESS**. This is the starting point. Great performers become calm, controlled and centered. Things seem to go 'slowly yet speedily.' Can you remember a time when you stayed calm during a crisis? What did you do to buy time? How can you follow these principles in the future? Looking ahead to the potential special moment, what can you do to stay calm?

- **CLARITY**. Great performers experience remarkable clarity during the special moments. Can you think of a time when this happened for you? Looking ahead to the potential special moment: How can you establish the real results to achieve? How can you get a clear picture of perfection?

- **CREATIVE SOLUTIONS**. Great performers then quickly go through (a) the 'conventional solutions' and (b) the 'creative solutions.' Have you ever been through such a creative process? What did you do right? How can you follow these paths in the future? Looking ahead to your special moment, describe how you can settle on your creative solution.

- **COMMITMENT**. Great performers then commit themselves to their chosen route. (Sometimes, of course, they pursue parallel options.) Have you ever done this in the past? How did you make the choice? Can you follow similar principles in the future? Looking ahead to your special moment, describe the specific things you can do to commit yourself to your chosen path.

- **CONCRETE RESULTS**. Great performers produce concrete results. They get the right balance between concentrating on the process and the prize. They stay positive and 'focus on the top, not the drop.' Can you remember a crucial time when you delivered the goods? What did you do right then? How can you follow these paths in the future? Looking ahead to your special moment, describe how you can deliver the required concrete results.

- **CLASS**. Great performers sometimes reach their goals by showing that touch of class. Different people show class in different ways. What are your preferred methods? How can you add to your repertoire? People often become selfless at special moments. Putting themselves in the background, they appear to do things simply, swiftly and successfully. They are able to relax, re-centre and refocus – then flow, focus and finish. Can you remember a time when you followed this process? What did you do right? How can you follow similar principles in the future?

- Let's consider the approach described in *Class Act Thinking*. Can you think of a difficult situation you may face in the future? Looking ahead to the potential difficulty, ask yourself: 'How would a Class Act behave in this situation?' How can you follow these principles in your own way? Make a specific action plan.

- Let's explore where you can use your 'A' talent. Recognizing what you do best is the 'What,' but 'How' can you put it into practice? There are at least three options. (1) Present role – describe the steps you can take to use your talent in your present role. (This may or may not be possible.) (2) Potential role – describe the steps you can take to craft a new role that will be a 'Win-Win' for both yourself and an employer. (3) Possible new audiences – describe the steps you can take to find or generate a new audience that will pay you for being a class act.

- How to find such a place? Let's return for a moment to the earlier exercise called *My Possible Niche.* The key is to focus on stimulation – especially the projects, people and places. What kind of project will be stimulating? What kind of people – colleagues or customers – will be stimulating? What kind of place – culture and environment – will be stimulating?

Let's explore where you can find potential sponsors. People buy people – so who do you know who might be interested in what you offer? Looking at each potential sponsor in turn – what challenges do they face? What is their picture of perfection? How can you help them to be successful? How can you reach out to such people? Bearing these options in mind, move onto an action plan. Describe the steps you can take to create the opportunities to be a class act.

- Finally: How can you continue to be a Class Act? Try tackling the exercise that invites you to make a Development Plan. Describe the specific steps you can take to keep improving in the areas of **Character, Competence, Consistency, Creativity** and **Class**.

Appendix 2

Suggested Reading

The following books explore themes related to becoming a Class Act. Some of the titles have been mentioned in my previous books, but are included here to give an overview.

Thomas Armstrong, *7 Kinds of Smart*

'Six years ago I quit my job as a learning disabilities specialist,' writes Thomas. 'I no longer believed in learning disabilities. It was then that I turned to the concept of learning differences as an alternative to learning disabilities.' Building on Howard Gardner's view of multiple intelligences, Thomas describes how each child is gifted in his or her own way. His book provides a treasure chest of ideas for enabling people to make better use of the talents. You can find out more about his work at: **www.thomasarmstrong.com/**

Sylvia Ashton-Warner, *Teacher*

Sylvia was a remarkable teacher who educated Maori children in the 1930s. She achieved great results by employing pioneering methods. Encouraging the children to start from their own daily vocabulary, she enabled them to develop a love of learning and, consequently, a love of reading and writing. Sylvia's autobiography shows how she translated her philosophy into action.

Warren Bennis and Patricia Ward Biederman, *Organising Genius: The Secrets Of Creative Collaboration*

What do great teams do right to perform exceptional work? 'Great groups start with great people. Great groups think they are on a mission from God. Great groups are full of talented people who can work together. Great groups make sure the right person has the right job. Great groups ship; they deliver the goods.' A fine book for anybody who wants to build a Super Team.

Philip L Berman & Connie Goldman, *The Ageless Spirit*

'Life begins at 40,' used to be the saying. The authors of *The Ageless Spirit* maintain that life really begins to blossom at 60. This inspiring book shows how older people can pass on their wisdom to future generations. Rollo May and Maggie Kuhn are among the many contributors who show how people can leave a valuable legacy.

Bill Beswick, *Focused for Football: Developing A Winning Mental Approach*

Sounds an odd choice? Perhaps, but it is one of the best books on sports psychology and the lessons can be applied to any field of work. Bill provides tips and techniques that people can use to make the best use of their talents. You can discover more about his work via: **www.footballmind-uk.com/**

Richard Bolles, *What Color is Your Parachute?*

Created over 30 years ago, the famous job-hunter's manual is now an annual best seller. Richard's approach to shaping your own destiny is now fully accepted, but his insights still provide much food for thought. A life-affirming book that is packed with practical ideas for building a positive future. You can find an online guide to Parachute at: **www.jobhuntersbible.com/**

Marcus Buckingham & Don Clifton, *Now Discover Your Strengths*

How do you perform world class work? Surely it is by concentrating on 'improving' your weaknesses. Not so, say the authors: it is by leveraging your talents. Marcus and Don have been at the forefront of The Strengths Revolution. Packed with data, tools and ideas, this book shows how people can capitalize on what they do best. You can find out more about a key tool they use, StrengthsFinder, via the web site: **http://gmj.gallup.com/book_center/strengthsfinder/**

Curt Coffman & Gabriel Molina, *Follow This Path*

Another book from The Gallup Organization. Following in the tradition of *First, Break All The Rules* and *Now, Discover Your Strengths*, it outlines the importance of recruiting for talent. The book highlights 34 talent themes. It also shows how people can be helped to develop by using twelve questions that Gallup call the Q12. The authors' key message, however, is that building on strengths improves the bottom line. They show how companies that implemented the principles delivered increased profits. Discover more by going to the Gallup home page and then searching for The Gallup Path. **www.gallup.com/**

Joseph Campbell & Diane K. Osborne (editor). *Joseph Campbell Companion: Reflections On The Art Of Living*

Recorded during a seminar in California, Diane Osborn has woven the themes together in a way that gives an overview of Joseph Campbell's work. The chapters cover such issues as relationships, 'following your bliss,' spirituality and, of course, The Heroic Journey. Good to read in conjunction with Christopher Vogler's book, which is mentioned later.

Jim Collins, *Good to Great*

'Get the right people on the bus, the wrong people off the bus and the right people in the right places on the bus,' says Jim Collins. Packed with research, this is prime reading for anybody who wants to build a successful organization. You can find out more about his work by visiting: **www.jimcollins.com/**

Mihaly Csikszentmihalyi. *Flow: The Psychology Of Optimal Experience*

Mihaly writes: 'We have all experienced times when, instead of being buffeted by anonymous forces, we do feel in control of our actions, masters of our own fate. On the rare occasions that it happens, we feel a sense of exhilaration, a deep sense of enjoyment that is long cherished and that becomes a landmark in memory for what life should be like. The best moments usually occur when a person's body or mind is stretched to its limits in a voluntary effort to accomplish something difficult and worthwhile. Optimal experience is therefore something that we make happen.' A fine book that provides lessons on how to perform at your best.

Viktor Frankl, *Man's Search for Meaning*

Viktor describes his harrowing journey through the Nazi concentration camps. He found that many of the survivors had something to live for beyond the immediate terror. They had a book to write, a relationship to rebuild or a dream to pursue. He writes: 'Man is not free from his conditions, but he is free to take a stand towards his conditions.' As a result of his experiences, Viktor created a form of therapy that enabled people to fulfill their meaning in life.

Sara Hall, *Drawn to the Rhythm: A Passionate Life Reclaimed*

Sara reclaimed her life by taking up single sculling. *Drawn To The Rhythm* describe the trials and triumphs she encountered on the journey. Freeing herself from a loveless marriage was painful. Sara's real freedom emerged, however, after relearning the joy of sculling-- rather than being in love national acclaim and winning medals. She now spends much of her time working with women over 35, helping them to create a blueprint for the second half of their lives. You can discover more about her work via: **www.sarahall.org**.

Paul Hawken, *Growing a Business*

Paul reached many budding entrepreneurs through his American Public Television series on this topic. He writes: 'Remember that in business you are never trying to 'beat' the competition. You are trying to give your customer something other than what they are receiving from the competition. It is a waste of time and energy trying to beat the competition because the customer doesn't care about that rivalry.' This practical book shows how to 'recreate something that has been lost' and use your imagination, rather than money, to achieve business success.

Barrie Hopson & Mike Scally, *Build Your Own Rainbow*

This classic book, updated in 1999, takes the readers on a personal and professional journey. Packed with practical tools, it enables people to discover their work values, plus identify their occupational and transferable skills. Looking into the future, *Rainbow* helps readers to find their most comfortable career pattern and create action plans.

It also offers a system for pursuing their personal development and finding courses built on the key themes outlined in the book.

Jim Loehr & Tony Schwartz, *The Power of Full Engagement: Managing Energy, Not Time.*

This book is an acquired taste. Some people love it, others find it too prescriptive. The gist is in the subtitle: Managing Energy, Not Time. The authors provide many practical tips for managing your physical, psychological and productive energy. You can find out more about their approach – and complete a self-assessment form – by visiting. **www.corporateathlete.com/**

Samuel Oliner, *Do Unto Others: Extraordinary Acts Of Ordinary People.*

Samuel starts the book by describing how, as a 12-year-old orphan, he was rescued by non-Jews in war-torn Poland. He then goes on to chronicle many other acts of altruism by people throughout history. Together with Pearl Oliner, Samuel also co-authored *The Altruistic Personality*. That ground-breaking book studied the moral values that motivated some 500,000 'rescuers' to protect Jews during the Holocaust. Both books demonstrate how human beings can behave with exceptional kindness, even in the midst of horror. The Oliner's believe that such acts of courage challenge each of us to develop the best in our nature.

Mike Pegg, *The Art of Mentoring, The Mentor's Book, The Magic of Work,* and *The Super Teams Book*

Mentors have one of the most rewarding jobs in the world. They help people to achieve their picture of perfection. *The Art Of Mentoring* provides a practical model that many organizations have used as the basis for their mentoring programs. *The Mentor's Book* offers tools that you can use to help people tackle many different kinds of challenges. It outlines seven approaches to mentoring. These are: Classic Mentoring, Career Mentoring, Change Curve Mentoring, Creative Teamwork Mentoring, Coaching & Mentoring, Conflict Resolution Mentoring and Class Act Mentoring.

How can you balance your soul work and salary work? *The Magic of Work* shows how you can follow your vocation, find the right vehicle and do valuable work. While not necessary to read if you are familiar with the exercises in the Class Act approach, it contains many practical tips on how to make a living doing what you love.

The Super Teams Book provides a model that has been shown to actually work in organizations. Super Teams build on their strengths, set specific goals and achieve success. They are based on 'similarity of spirit' and 'diversity of strengths' – diversity of spirit is a recipe for disaster. They also have the right balance of Soul Players and Star Players – they have no Semi-Detached Players. Packed with exercises, the book has been used by many teams that have achieved their picture of perfection.

More details about Mike's work can be found at: **www.thestrengthscompany.com**

Victoria Lynn Schmidt, *45 Master Characters*

Would you like to understand peoples' character? Psychology books give an insight – but you may be able to learn even more from literature, plays and films. Produced primarily for writers, Victoria's book provides a crash course in understanding different personality types. Starting from the Mythic Models, it outlines the strengths and limitations of each character. You may be familiar with Joseph Campbell's work on 'The Heroic Journey'; Victoria's book also outlines 'The Heroine's Journey.' Well worth reading.

Martin Seligman, *Authentic Happiness*

After qualifying as a psychologist, Martin spent many years studying how people could change by fixing the areas in which they failed. At a certain point, however, he realized that people could also grow by focusing on their strengths. This led to him co-founding The Positive Psychology Network. Based on research, this approach enables people to find and nurture their strengths. One key point to note – he uses the term 'strengths' to refer to personality characteristics, such as wisdom. He uses the term 'talents' to refer to natural gifts, such as the ability to sing in perfect pitch. More about his work, plus a self-assessment form, can be found at: **www.authentichappiness.org/**

Al Siebert, *The Survivor Personality*

What can we learn from survivors? Al Siebert identifies the characteristics of people who have overcome tremendous setbacks. Many of his findings, including the concept of Personal Radar, can be applied to our personal and professional lives. One of the best of the 'survivor' books on the market. More about his work can be found at: www.thrivenet.com/

Christopher Vogler, *The Writer's Journey: Mythic Structure For Storytellers & Screenwriters*

Christopher's book shows how film plots often follow the structure that Joseph Campbell found in myths and legends. The Heroic Journey is also followed by people who embark on their personal odyssey. Christopher writes: 'A hero leaves her comfortable, ordinary surroundings to venture into a challenging, unfamiliar world. It may be an outward journey to an actual place: a labyrinth, forest or cave, a strange city or country, a new locale that becomes the arena for her conflict with antagonistic, challenging forces. But there are many stories that take the hero on an inward journey, one of the mind, the heart, the spirit. In any good story the hero grows and changes, making a journey from one way of being to the next: from despair to hope, weakness to strength, folly to wisdom, love to hate, and back again. It's these emotional journeys that hook an audience and make a story worth watching.' People may go through similar stages on the route towards becoming a class act.

The Fast Company Magazine

Many people prefer to keep abreast with events by reading magazines. Everybody has their own favorites. *The Fast Company* is one that often stays ahead of the game. You can get a taste by visiting their web site at: **www.fastcompany.com/homepage/index.html**

CONTACTS

If you are interested in any of the themes in my books, please contact me directly.

The best way is via email at:

mike@thestrengthscompany.com

You will also find more exercises on the website at: www.thestrengthscompany.com.

Another key contact is Sue Moore, an outstanding mentor. You can find out more about her superb work on:

www.amadeusnetwork.com

Sue can be reached at:

sue@amadeus.prestel.co.uk

I also know many other people who do outstanding work in the field of mentoring, career development and helping people to build super teams.

Contact me if you would like more information.

Mike Pegg

Index

The items listed below in CAPITALS refer to the exercises found throughout the book

Comments about this book

'Many organizations are now focusing on enabling people to develop their talents. Mike's book gives people a great framework for identifying the passion and path they can follow to capitalize on their strengths. Some people may find the book challenging. Why? It will remind them of what they must do to put themselves in the position to be successful. Sometimes it is easy to get side-tracked by following other's expectations, rather than being true to oneself and one's own talents. The Class Act Book outlines practical steps and processes that people can follow towards fully utilizing their talents--and, in the long-run, this will benefit both themselves and their organization.'

Roy White, Vice President, Human Resources, Sony Europe.

'All of us know people who are good at what they do – but how many do you know that are EXCEPTIONAL at what they do? It's the last 5% of effort and professionalism that turns the merely good into great. Mike has an uncanny ability to simplify how to gain the elusive edge that transforms your performance and earning potential.'

Katie Ledger, Newscaster, Five News

'Many of us spend many years discovering our 'A' talent. Certainly the journey is rewarding, but sometimes we could use a short cut! The Class Act Book provides many tools you can use to find your own and other peoples' top talents. It offers a great pack of resources for anybody who wants to become a class act.'

Amanda Mackenzie, Director Group Marketing, BT

Over the years I have had the privilege of working with many fine people in charity fund-raising and business. Like great actors, singers and athletes, the high performers have had two characteristics in common. First, they have consistently delivered at least an 8/10. Second, they have added a touch of class that has helped them – and their teams – to reach 10/10. Mike's book provides many models and tools that people can use to develop their talents and aim for the perfect ten.

Bill Grimsey, Chief Executive, The Big Food Group

CPSIA information can be obtained at www.ICGtesting.com
Printed in the USA
BVOW080453290911

272157BV00005B/9/P

9 781611 100228